D0345268

The 13th Gift

The 13th Gift

A TRUE STORY
of a CHRISTMAS MIRACLE

Joanne Huist Smith

HARMONY
BOOKS • NEW YORK

Published in the United States by Harmony Books, an imprint of the Crown Publishing Group, a division of Random House LLC, a Penguin Random House Company, New York.

www.crownpublishing.com

Harmony Books is a registered trademark, and the Circle colophon is a trademark of Random House LLC.

Library of Congress Cataloging-in-Publication Data
Smith, Joanne Huist.
The 13th gift : a true story of a Christmas miracle / by Joanne Huist Smith.
pages cm
1. Christmas—Anecdotes. 2. Kindness—Anecdotes. 3. Miracles—Anecdotes. 4. Smith, Joanne Huist. 5. Smith, Joanne Huist—Family. I. Title. II. Title: Thirteenth gift.
BV45.S484 2014
394.2663—dc23
2014015048

ISBN 978-0-553-41855-2
eBook ISBN 978-0-553-41856-9

PRINTED IN THE UNITED STATES OF AMERICA

Book design by Anna Thompson
Illustrations by Julia Rothman
Jacket design by Nupoor Gordon
Jacket photography by Ttatty/Shutterstock, pkline/iStock, Tsekhmister/iStock, claudio.arnese/iStock

10 9 8

First Edition

For Rick, my very first true friend, and our three most precious gifts, Benjamin, Nicholas, and Megan.

On the twelfth day of Christmas,
my true love sent to me
Twelve drummers drumming,
Eleven pipers piping,
Ten lords a-leaping,
Nine ladies dancing,
Eight maids a-milking,
Seven swans a-swimming,
Six geese a-laying,
Five golden rings,
Four calling birds,
Three French hens,
Two turtle doves,
And a partridge in a pear tree!

Contents

Foreword

Dear Readers,

I learned the lyrics to "The Twelve Days of Christmas" carol as a kid in grammar school choir, when the magic of the holiday season still filled me with a sense of wonder and possibility, a dreams-come-true mentality. Partridges and pear trees, ladies dancing and leaping lords—I had thought the words of the tune farcical. I didn't know then that the key to happiness was hidden within its silly stanzas.

I had spent my life grasping at those five golden rings: a husband, three healthy children, and a comfortable home. Then just before Christmas in 1999, my beloved husband died in the night, and I realized my gold was fragile as glass.

We were shattered.

I found no comfort or joy in the approaching holidays, only memories that cut at my heart like broken pieces of a treasured Christmas ornament.

I stopped singing. It hurt even to breathe. I wanted to banish the holidays from our lives. But then something extraordinary happened.

Thirteen days before Christmas, gifts began appearing at my home. They were just small tokens of the holiday season, accompanied by a card with lines similar to the carol. Each was signed simply, "Your true friends." At first, I resisted the intrusion of Christmas into my grief. But slowly, as the gifts kept arriving, my heart began to thaw. The gifts made my children smile, got us talking, as we tried to identify the source of our mysterious presents. They were teaching us how to function as a family again.

The romantic in me would like to believe a miracle touched my family that Christmas, and in a way that is true. But I know that the miracle was the way a small act of kindness saved my family and brought us back to each other. Years later, the magic of the holiday season is still colored by the light that those friends shone into our lives. Thinking of what a powerful impact those anonymous gifts made on my family has changed the way I see the holidays—not just as an excuse to give and receive presents with my loved ones, but as a time when it is more important than ever to step outside of my own world and consider those around me, to open my heart, reach out my hand, and engage. The holidays are a time to rejoice, to remember, to reflect on seasons past, and to celebrate our memories. This book is about finding a way to honor those who cannot be with us this season, to create new and joyful memories, to experience this season of giving in a very special way.

Come.

Walk with me.

I will share with you the message that forever changed my family, the healing magic of the 13th Gift.

The 13th Gift

Chapter One
The First Day of Christmas

Just before dawn on December 13, my daughter, Megan, tugs at my nightshirt.

"Mom, we missed the school bus."

Disoriented and still half asleep, I start calling commands to my children before my feet hit the floor.

"Splash water on your face! Get dressed! We've got bananas and granola bars in the kitchen for breakfast. I'll get the car heated up, but we have to leave in ten minutes!"

Megan dashes off as directed, while I rouse her less cooperative brothers.

When I hear movement in all of their bedrooms, I take a two-minute bath, swipe on makeup, and pummel my hair with baby powder to give it poof. A dark suit hanging on the back of the bathroom door becomes my ensemble for the day. The vision in the mirror is not enchanting, but at least my red eyes and rumpled clothes seem to match.

"I dare anyone to criticize," I say, pointing at my reflection.

I check on the readiness of my three Smiths—Megan, ten; Nick, twelve; and Ben, seventeen—dig car keys from my purse, and toss four coats onto the couch.

"Two minutes," I holler. "Everybody outside."

I whisper a plea for even a few weak rays of sunshine as I open the front door, but instead I meet typical weather for Bellbrook, Ohio, less than two weeks before Christmas: gray, wet, and cold. It has always been the warmth of the people, our neighbors, the community, mooring us to this southern suburb of Dayton. But this December, I only feel the chill.

In my haste to heat up the car, I nearly knock over a poinsettia sitting outside our front door. Raindrops on its holiday wrapper sparkle in the porch light.

"What the heck?"

Megan peeks around me, and her face lights up.

"It's so pretty!"

That's my Meg: ever hopeful even after we've been through so much. I wish I could be more like her, but then again, I'm not ten.

"Yes, real pretty. Where are your brothers? Get your brothers."

"Where did it come from, Mom? Let's bring it in."

I stand at the door watching the cold rain beat down on the plant's four blood-red blooms. For me, bringing the flower into the house offers as much appeal as inviting in a wet, rabid dog for the holidays. I absolutely understand Scrooge now. I want to go to bed tonight and wake up on December 26. No shopping. No baking. No tree with lights. I'm not in a mood to make memories. The ones I have just hurt; I can't imagine new ones will feel any better. I don't expect to avoid the holiday altogether. I merely hope to minimize the affair as much as possible. Christmas is supposed to be about family, and ours has a larger-than-life-sized hole. The flower can't fill it.

I imagine my husband standing next to the closet he lined with shelves last December. Beside him, our fully trimmed Canadian fir stands in a growing puddle of pine needles.

"You're killing the Christmas tree," I scolded, pointing to the mounting evidence on the floor. He tested my theory with a whack of his hammer on the closet shelf. Needles pirouetted from the branches.

"At least these shelves aren't going anywhere," he said. "Neither am I."

So why am I alone?

I search for him in the shadows of the house in the hours between good-night kisses and the morning alarm, even though I know he's not there. My back throbs from the continual jabbing of a broken coil in the sofa, but I can't bring myself to sleep upstairs in the bed we shared. I won't even shift to his side of the sofa.

The space Rick filled, it's empty.

Megan needs Christmas, but I'm not ready to descend into fa-la-la land. The appearance of this flower is sure to jump-start the nagging about buying a Christmas tree and scavenging through boxes in the basement for our collection of Santa Claus figurines. I consider asking Rick's brother Tom and his wife, Charlotte, to let the kids spend the holidays with them, just a day or two. I could hide from the season while they shower my children with gifts and stuff them with turkey and banana pudding. The kids would only be a few miles away if I got needy, but

I could delegate the Christmas trimmings to Tom and Char. Delivery of the idea will be tricky. I can hear the chorus of "No way," and recognize my voice as the loudest. I don't want the holidays, but I do want my kids home with me.

The clock on the mantel chimes seven a.m., and I snap back into my "single mom with children nearly late for school" mode.

"I don't know where the flower came from, Meg. But I'm not bringing it in. It's wet, and the potting soil looks like a mudslide."

"But, Mom, it's a Christmas flower."

Megan presses her plea for the plant, as Ben walks up the steps from his basement bedroom. I know he was out until nearly three a.m., and I'm not fool enough to believe he was studying. He doesn't give me a chance to say good morning or to question him about the missed curfew.

"I don't see why I have to go to school. Most of my friends have already left town for winter break."

The thought of having this conversation, again, makes me weary. I want to crawl back under the covers and tell him to do the same, but it's not an option for either of us.

"Just get your coat. You've already missed too many days of school."

Megan stands between us.

"Look, Ben. Look what we found on the porch."

I'm not sure why or exactly when, but she has become the peacemaker of the family in the last two months.

"Where'd it come from?"

Ben moves past me to retrieve the flower. I put a hand up to stop him.

"Whoa." Ben throws his arms up in surrender, but his eyes

warn me a battle is brewing. I know there are words to soothe him, but they aren't in my vocabulary this morning.

"Please, just go get your book bag."

Ben disappears back down the basement stairs just as Nick leaps down three steps at a time from his bedroom upstairs. Megan draws him into the poinsettia debate.

"Mom doesn't want to bring it in, but I think we should. It's too cold outside for a such a pretty little flower."

Nick glances out the door and immediately loses interest.

"Better not bring it in," he whispers to Meg. "Might be a bomb disguised as a flower. Yeah. It's probably okay as long as it's outside where the temperature is nearly freezing, but bring it into a warm house and *kaboom*!"

Megan jumps. "Mom!"

"Okay. Okay. I'll bring it in." I acquire several fingernails full of wet potting soil, and muddy raindrops mark a trail across the living room carpet to the kitchen.

"Shit."

"Don't say that," Megan scolds. "Hey, there's something else."

Megan follows me into the kitchen carrying a plastic bag with a homemade Christmas card inside. The note is written on yellow parchment with ripped edges, giving it an aged look. Someone has penned the message in an elegant cursive hand and sketched a holly leaf in the corner. The verse is a familiar one, though some of the lines are different:

On the first day of Christmas
your true friends give to you,
one Poinsettia for all of you.

Megan converts the note to song and starts dancing around the kitchen. Our blue-eyed Siberian husky, Bella, begins howling in unison. Nick grabs the parchment.

"What friends? Was it Aunt Char? Uncle Tom? Someone from school? A teacher maybe?"

I can't answer him.

Right now, I don't feel as if we have any friends. Telephone calls to chat and make plans for weekend gatherings have stopped. There are no Christmas cards in our mailbox, only bills.

Ben takes advantage of the commotion to announce he is not going to school.

"I've got a headache. I'm going back to bed."

I want to put my arms around Ben and tell him that I understand his need to banish that song and everything relating to the holidays from our lives, but I don't have the energy. Instead, I think of their father's voice, bellowing the loudest when we sang that same carol as he drove us to a Christmas tree farm just outside of Yellow Springs.

After nearly twenty years of marriage, I had grown accustomed to Rick's often off-key chorus, but still I had been grateful for the closed truck windows. At the tree lot, we had meandered down rows of Scotch and white pines, Canadian firs, and blue spruce. Megan begged for one of each. Nick set his heart on a fifteen-footer, though our family room is only twelve feet tall, floor to ceiling. Ben's only request was that the tree branches be sparse near the bottom.

"More room for presents," he had explained.

Together, we had selected the perfect tree, then Rick had shooed the kids and me back into the warm truck to share a thermos of hot chocolate that I'd made for the occasion and brought with us. He alone braved temperatures in the low twenties, chipping away at the stubborn tree trunk with a dull ax. Wearing a red-and-black flannel shirt, dark jeans, and knit cap, he had looked like a lumberjack as he dragged the tree to the truck, strong, healthy, and rugged but with adorable rosy cheeks.

That was my man.

Standing six feet five, with wavy black hair and hands large enough to schlep an eight-pound infant in his palm like a pizza, Rick had reveled in his role of protector, provider, "the Big Dad." He always had his huge arms wrapped around us.

The clock on the mantel chimes again, reminding me how late we really are. Meanwhile the poinsettia is creating a puddle of dirty water on the counter, forging a channel down the kitchen cabinet onto the floor. I pick up the pot, shiny paper and all, and toss it into the sink. It topples and splatters damp potting soil on the clean dishes left to drain after last night's dinner.

"Shit. Shit. Shit. Everybody in the car," I shout.

"Mommy . . ." Megan huffs, stomping her foot on the floor.

"I know. I know. Don't say that."

Megan straightens the plant before collecting her backpack and heading out to the car. Her brothers and I follow. The car is cold.

I deposit the still grumbling Ben at the high school and navigate through a jumble of parent traffic at the junior high that Nick attends.

"Learn something," I call as he slams the car door. He just keeps walking.

Megan, who attends the intermediate school, starts classes later than her brothers, so she and I sit in the car for twenty minutes practicing her spelling words, all holiday related, of course.

"Ornament. *O-r-n-a-m-e-n-t*. Ornament. Poinsettia. *P-o-i-n-s-e-t-t-i-a*. Poinsettia. Do you think . . . do you suppose Daddy could've left it for us, Mom? You know, the *p-o-i-n-s-e-t-t-i-a*."

She looks at me with chocolate eyes so like her Dad's, but there's a new yearning haunting them that wasn't there until two months ago. I want to tell her that his love lingers all around us, but how can I say that if I'm not sure it's true? Do I lie? It's easier to stick to safe topics like school, basketball practice, and her Girl Scout troop.

She needs reassurance from me that we'll be okay, but I'm not sure we will.

"What I think is that it's time for you to go to class and earn a few A's," I say, pulling up the zipper on her bright yellow jacket. I plant a kiss on top of her head.

"Put your hood up, because . . ."

"Body heat escapes off your head." We say it together and laugh.

She starts up the sidewalk toward the school but turns and runs back to the car. I check the seat to see what she's forgotten, but it's empty. Megan presses her nose against the car window just as I am about to roll it down. Her breath leaves a puff of steam on the glass.

"Can we get a Christmas tree this weekend, Mom? Please? Okay, great," she says, without waiting for an answer.

"Maybe once you clean your room!" I call after her weakly, but she is already running toward the school. She waves before disappearing inside, taking what's left of my heart with her.

Before I get the car into gear, tears are blurring my vision.

On my way to the office, I weave through town past Christmas decorations dangling from lampposts in the shopping plaza. By the time I reach the entrance ramp to the interstate, I feel like screaming.

I pound the steering wheel and accidentally hit the horn. An elderly gentleman in a black sedan pulls over into the slow lane, and I speed up guiltily. I am ashamed of my actions now, and of the sense of panic that moved into our home when Rick left us.

I am terrified of the growing cache of bills stowed out of sight in the kitchen drawer. The electric company has demanded a deposit, even though Rick and I have had an account with them for twenty years. The account, of course, was in his name. My name was unknown to most of our creditors, but they are learning it now.

My friend Kate tells me Rick is at peace. He is in a place where there is no pain, no worry, no angst, but I imagine Rick crazy angry with God. That steel-melting emotion burns in me, too. I can't explain to the kids why this has happened, why other families have fathers and theirs doesn't. I can't tell them that I wish it had been me who died because Rick would know how to help them through this.

A driver hardly old enough to have a license lays on his horn, and I realize my car is straddling the dotted line between two lanes.

"Jesus, Jo, pay attention," I say to myself, then mouth "sorry" to the kid, who responds with a flash of his middle finger. I consider returning the gesture, but my heart isn't in it. I am grateful to him for riveting my attention back to the road.

By now I can feel warm air shooting from the vents of the car heater, but I am still shivering.

What would happen to the kids if something happened to me?

Over the last few weeks, I've come to fear every pain and sore muscle. Sometimes, I get nervous just walking the dog.

"You're being paranoid," I say out loud, and then realize I am still talking to myself. I think the driver in the tan truck in the lane to the left notices.

"I'm not nuts," I shout at the window. The driver speeds up.

"Yeah, that's right. Get outta my way."

Behind the closed car window I feel a pinch of bravado until I realize I am doing that talking-to-myself thing again.

Music. Turn on the radio.

I tune into 99.9 FM, hoping for a happy song.

"Chestnuts roasting on an open fire . . ." Anne Murray's voice fills the car.

"Not helping," I tell the radio.

So I switch the station, then again, and again, finally just turning it off two miles down the road. Every song, even ones I've never heard before, reminds me of Rick.

It's a relief to find the parking lot empty in front of the *Dayton Daily News* bureau, where I work. I grab a tissue from a stash in the glove box and try to repair my eye makeup. I have time to close my eyes and recuperate from the drive, time enough to get rid of my red eyes and reapply makeup before going inside.

Despite the chaos of the morning, I am still one of the first people to arrive. One by one, coworkers fill the office. We are a busy group, especially with the holidays approaching and everyone hoping to finish their work quickly and head out to holiday shop for their loved ones. I wonder if someone in the office thought to shop for my family this year and might be behind the poinsettia. I mention the mysterious morning gift, but no one seems interested. That makes me suspicious. In the newsroom, there's no such thing as a question that doesn't have an answer. My reporter brain immediately suspects that there must be a reason that nobody else seems curious about my mystery flower. Is it because they already know who left it?

Joann Rouse, a fellow reporter, is the last to arrive. She had hovered around me at Rick's funeral, standing close, offering tissues when needed. In the weeks since, she has coerced me out of the office several times for lunch on the pretext of brainstorming story ideas. She always guides the conversation back to my family. I never know how to answer her queries about the kids, the house, how I'm doing. The meal usually ends in tears, both hers and mine.

At least she cares enough to ask.

Leaving an anonymous gift seems like something she might do. As I tell her about the poinsettia, I watch closely for her reaction.

"Maybe whoever sent it will own up on Christmas," she says, punching in the telephone number to retrieve her voice mail.

Not the reaction I expected from a coworker presented with a Christmas mystery.

She's a reporter.

We're nosey.

"She must be behind that stupid flower," I tell myself.

Coaxing her to fess up to leaving the gift will take finesse. I ease into the interrogation after she hangs up the phone.

"Started your Christmas shopping yet?" I ask.

Joann winces and rolls her eyes.

"Not yet. Maybe this weekend," she says casually, glancing at her computer as she watches it boot up.

My coworker seems suspiciously anxious to attack a story assignment. She's thumbing through a notepad that I am pretty sure is blank. I press on with an additional question.

"Have you checked out any of the Christmas tree lots in town? Megan has been bugging me to buy one."

Joann's attitude transforms.

"The lot up the street has gorgeous trees. I stopped there last night to buy a wreath. They had the largest poinsettias I have ever seen."

"Poinsettias, really?" I ask. "And did you happen to buy one for a coworker?"

But instead of confessing, Joann laughs.

"Just enjoy the flower, Jo. Doesn't matter who left it."

Oh, but it does. And I have figured it out.

Confident that I have discovered the identity of our "true friends," I set aside worries about the kids, and all thought of Christmas, to tackle a school-funding story. For a few hours, I am not a widow or a mother. I gratefully surrender those roles, even if only for a while.

Just after three thirty, the kids start calling. Megan is the first. She is home and has washed the red foil wrapping on the poinsettia with an old washcloth and dish soap.

"Looks tie-dyed," she announces. "I like it."

"What looks tie-dyed, the wrapping or the washcloth?" I ask.

"Both," she giggles. "I've got Girl Scouts today. Can you pick me up at six thirty?"

Ten minutes later, Nick is on the phone.

"Wrestling practice until seven thirty. Don't forget, it's in the school gym."

"I'll be there. I promise."

Forty-five minutes pass before I hear from Ben.

"Megan said we're getting a Christmas tree this weekend. I'm busy."

"I'm not sure when we'll do it."

"Doesn't matter," Ben says. "I'm busy all weekend."

I begin to worry about getting my story edited and myself out of the office in time to pick up all the kids and get dinner ready. I finally wrap up at work at six twenty, leaving ten minutes to make the half-hour trip back to Bellbrook. I drive home at a much faster pace than the trip to the office this morning, but I start to panic as I shave the clock close. I have never left a kid waiting in the cold.

Megan is standing outside the school with several friends when I drive up. She is smiling. I am not the last mom to arrive.

"Look what we made at Girl Scouts."

From a piece of red yarn, she dangles a Christmas tree ornament fashioned from construction paper and wooden sticks: a poinsettia.

"It's for our Christmas tree," she says, as if I needed to be reminded.

Chapter Two

The Second Day of Christmas

For weeks, my sister-in-law Charlotte has been chiding me to hustle up my holiday preparations.

"You have got to give those kids a Christmas," has become her latest trope.

This morning, she calls before six a.m., offering to pick up Nick and Megan from their sports practices to provide me with a few hours of shopping time after work.

"Just get it over with," she insists. "You love Christmas shopping. Getting out there might cheer you up."

I have no confidence in her logic, but I agree to give it a try.

That is how I find myself waiting with my turn signal on for a mom and a toddler to move past an open parking space in the shopping plaza, when a gray-haired grandpa type whips his Lexus around them and nabs my spot. The mom jerks her cart back to avoid a collision.

"Asshole," she shouts, covering her daughter's ears with gloved hands.

"Merry Christmas," the old guy hollers as he steps from his car. He winks at me as he passes. I want to shove his smug expression somewhere distinctly un-Christmasy, but he's already vaulting through the store doors. I've never been much of a musician, but I imagine rewriting the lyrics to "Silver Bells." In my more realistic version, people are meeting "scowl after scowl" instead of "smile after smile."

I abandon my search for a primo parking place, and drive to the adjacent shopping center where most of the businesses are closed for the day.

As I enter the store, strains of "Frosty the Snowman" blasting over the sound system weaken my resolve. Though my intent is to buy a mountain bike for Nick, I veer first into Rick's favorite department, hardware. The layout of the aisles here is as familiar to me as housewares. Before Rick tackled a home repair—turning our concrete-walled basement into a playroom, building a deck on the back of the house, or crafting a ceramic-tiled counter for the kitchen—he would drag the whole family with him to the hardware department to select supplies. I am struck with the idea of buying some sort of useful tool that I can donate in Rick's name to the Salvation Army or Habitat for Humanity.

There must have been some magic
in that old silk hat they found.

I don't ever remember hearing Christmas music in this section of the store before, but the lines of "Frosty" are loud enough to rattle the light fixtures. I imagine ending the iceman's romp through town with a blowtorch, or at the very least barbecuing the store's sound system. It's cruel, but the thought makes me laugh at myself.

"Do you carry acetylene torches?" I ask a clerk.

Thumpity, thump, thump. Thumpity, thump, thump, look at Frosty go.

I load the torch into my shopping cart, thinking that this could be a useful donation or perhaps a Christmas gift for my brother-in-law Tom. Maybe I'll keep it for myself. A more likely scenario, there won't be presents or a tree to put them under at our house on December 25.

Just buy a bike. One step at a time.

On my trek to the toy department, I toss wrapping paper, gift cards, and tape into the cart. My holiday purchases, so far, are limited to bags of athletic socks and underwear for each of the kids—the only two items Rick ever asked for on his Christmas list. When we first met, Rick didn't understand my need to ferret out the perfect gift for each loved one. His mother had died when he was three years old, and the holidays never took on much significance in his family. The Christmas gifts he received thereafter had been mostly functional . . . until he met me. It took time for him to catch my enthusiasm for the holidays. Maybe I just wore him down. The year I bought him a video camera, he waited two full days to open it as a protest over the expense. I caught him reading the manual the next day, and by New Year's Eve he threatened to leave the tool-and-die industry to make movies. He gave me a nightgown that year, a twin to one I already owned.

The following year, he bought me a sterling silver necklace and matching bracelet.

I understand now why his dad was not a fan of holiday shopping. It feels as if I'm betraying my husband to even think about celebrating the holidays. All I want for Christmas is him, and the idea of making new holiday memories without Rick just makes me miss him more. I just can't operate under the same modus operandi as past years, and I have no idea how I'm supposed to behave.

"I need a damn rule book."

My lament is loud enough to summon a clerk.

"In the video department," she responds, pointing to the rear of the store, apparently ignoring my profanity in a way that my daughter does not. "Books are back by the videos."

I move in that direction, embarrassed to have been caught talking to myself. I hope the clerk will chalk my behavior up to temporary holiday insanity and not a more general affliction. I glance backward to see if she is occupied with another customer. That's when I really do get into an accident. I smack into a life-sized, blow-up lawn Santa with my shopping cart; he doesn't deflate, but he is wobbling close to a display of glass candle globes.

"Can I help you?"

Now I have the clerk's undivided attention, and she is looking none too surprised to see that I am the cause of the near display disaster.

"My daughter would love him," I say weakly.

"Then buy one."

Abashed, I grab a blow-up Santa and toss him in my cart next to the torch.

I know our house looks cheerless compared to others on the

block dressed in white lights, nativity scenes, and grazing wire reindeer. Trimming the outside of the house was Rick's bailiwick, not mine. I am not going to buy this blow-up, but I don't want to put the Santa back on the shelf with the clerk now stalking my every move. Under her now watchful eye, I pretend to consider buying hand-painted ornaments, a quilted Christmas tree skirt, metal tins with snowy scenes on the lids, and others filled with assortments of chocolates.

None of the items appeal to me.

I do want to feel the Christmas tug that usually consumes me this time of year. I have always begun holiday shopping before Thanksgiving and usually have a trove of presents purchased long before the onslaught of the holiday stampede. Then I purposefully forget how much I have spent and buy more just to be part of the holiday rush. I used to love crowded shopping malls, wrapping presents, baking cookies, the swarm of family visiting on Christmas Eve.

Not anymore.

For the first time in nearly twenty years, my husband isn't standing beside me mentally calculating our seasonal checkbook damage, and I have no will to spend.

Wouldn't Rick find this ironic.

When the sales clerk starts humming along to "Winter Wonderland," I leave the Christmas displays and head over to toys, taking the blow-up Santa with me.

Just buy the bike and get out of here, I tell myself.

The toy aisles are humming with dads and moms and grandparents flitting from Barbie dolls to board games. I pause near the video games, looking for anything to jump out at me.

Rick and I had decided years ago we weren't bringing a video-

game system into the house. We wanted our kids to fill their free time with more educational activities, like reading. Then I had gone on a weekend trip to Christmas shop in Frankenmuth, Michigan, with my mom and sisters.

I was only gone three days, but when I returned, we owned a Nintendo. With controller in hand, Rick was seated on the family room floor, gyrating right, then left, sitting up tall, slouching, unconsciously mimicking the movements of Super Mario on the television screen. The kids were gathered around him like little apostles, moving as he moved in a choreographed dance.

They never heard me walk in the door.

"It's a science experiment," Rick insisted before I flicked the back of his head with an American Girl book I had purchased for Megan.

Now, three years later, our collection of video-game systems also includes a Nintendo Game Boy, Sega Game Gear, and numerous computer games that the kids play together. Since his father's death, Nick has become completely immersed in these escape pods that draw him into video worlds where beaten and bloodied avatars spring back to life with each new game. I don't want to encourage the habit, but I can see that the games are helping him cope.

I venture into the video-game aisle, where I find the old guy who stole my parking space in a spat over a game with the mom and toddler he nearly hit.

"I saw it first," the old guy shouts.

"I just went to get someone to unlock the display case," the mother fires back. "They're paging a clerk for *me*."

I should keep walking, but I don't.

"Let her have it, you old grump."

The two turn and look at me. The old guy's face glows Christmas red, and the mom stands with fists balled like she's ready to duke it out, either with him or with me. Another voice joins in the fray.

"You again."

I don't have to turn around to identify its owner. It's that same sales clerk. Instead of defusing the fighters, she's coming at me.

"I thought you were looking for books."

"Well . . . a bike actually."

"Three aisles down. On the left. How about you go have a look."

I flash my best mean face at the old guy and leave the aisle with a final, menacing remark.

"Give the game to the girl."

My legs are shaking by the time I reach the bicycle racks. There is less foot traffic here; bikes aren't a big seller in the Midwest in winter. I am grateful for the quiet, but it doesn't last long.

"Can I help you, ma'am?" a stock boy asks as I browse ten-speeds.

"Yes," I say, gesturing between a trendy yellow and a traditional blue mountain bike. "I just can't decide on the color."

I want to buy the bike. I intend to buy the bike, but before I make a decision, Bing Crosby is crooning the opening lines of "I'll Be Home for Christmas," and my mind erases every thought except that Rick will not be with me to assemble the bicycle on Christmas Eve. When the stock boy clears his throat to get my attention, I jump.

"I'm sick of Christmas music," I bark at the young man, who

is not much older than my Ben. I am ashamed as soon as the words leap off my tongue, but it's too late to take them back.

"Yeah, Christmas sucks," he says mildly, reversing down the aisle. A couple dressed in matching holiday sweatshirts glare at me.

"Just kidding," I mumble at them, and I flee.

I abandon my cart with the blow-up Santa, wrapping paper, tape, and the torch, and seek the privacy of the public restroom. I feel safe behind the hollow metal walls of the stall, where flushing toilets and humming hand dryers muffle the store music. But they don't silence the memories inside my head. I lean against the door and close my eyes, willing the accusations to stop.

Looking back, I know Rick's body tried to warn me. The tightening of his belt by two notches, the change in his complexion from olive to ashen, and his hands, especially his hands. Hands that had held mine since age nineteen, that balanced our newborns in their massive palms, built dies and decks and repaired kids' toys. Those hands were trying to tell me something was wrong with their thin, loose skin. I just didn't want to hear it.

A cardiologist had tried multiple medications and procedures to coerce Rick's rapid heartbeat into a normal rhythm. On a late September morning at Miami Valley Hospital, a technician had even stopped Rick's heart in the hope it would restart itself at a normal pace. Rick needed surgery to replace a leaky heart valve, a birth defect that could no longer just be monitored at age forty-five. We could have scheduled the surgery immediately, but Rick wanted to postpone it.

"Can I wait a few weeks?" he asked the doctor. "I want to time my recovery with the kids' Christmas vacation."

I dig a thumbnail into the palm of my hand until it bleeds.

The pain makes me feel better, slows the rapid pace of my heart. I can handle this kind of pain. I dab at the blood with a wad of toilet paper, thinking how I would freak out if one of my kids did this.

I imagine spending the rest of my life in the store bathroom. I can see the headline: MOTHER BECOMES RESTROOM RECLUSE.

"Mommy, I have to go to the bathroom," a little voice whines outside my stall. "I've got to go *now*."

A mop of red curls peeks under my door.

What am I doing in here?

It takes me a few minutes to summon the nerve to open the door. I exit the bathroom just behind my stall peeper and her mother. A tall man with carrot-colored hair sweeps the child up into his arms and my heart aches.

"Ready to go see Santa?" he asks.

I walk past the family with my head bowed, hoping the child doesn't mention me to her daddy. While the family gets in line for a photo with Santa, I backtrack to the bike aisle to retrieve my shopping cart. My stalker clerk has beaten me to it. She is holding the blow-up Santa in one-hand and talking to the bicycle stock boy.

"There was something strange about that lady," I hear her saying.

"For sure. Who doesn't like Christmas music?"

I sneak out of the aisle. The crush of shoppers seems to be multiplying as I head toward the exit, and it's difficult to maneuver through the crowded departments, even without a shopping cart. People are grabbing merchandise off shelves as if their lives depend on buying this gift or that.

"Won't Cindy love this doll?"

"How about a tie for Uncle George, or maybe slippers?"

"Grandma needs a new robe."

Their enthusiasm defeats me.

I spot the old guy, mom, and toddler in a checkout lane on my way to the door. They appear to have reconciled and are talking to each other, laughing. Both hold a copy of the video game. Their smiling faces somehow manage to annoy me even more.

Back in the car, I navigate to the nearest drive-through restaurant, order two hot fudge cakes with extra whipped cream, pull into a parking space, and devour them both in the dark. The food comforts me. It's something I can control. I go back through the line for two double-decker cheeseburgers with extra pickle. By the time I gobble down the last bite of my fast-food feast, I am late for my rendezvous with the kids. I head out to my sister-in-law's house with a black hole in the trunk of my car where presents should be. By the time I pull into Tom and Char's driveway, the fudge cakes and burgers are warring in my stomach, incited by a full on attack of failure. I dread facing Charlotte.

She meets me at the door with a hopeful look.

"Did you buy a bike?"

I don't want to lie to her, but I also don't want to tell her the truth.

"They didn't have the right color . . . checking other stores."

The expression on Char's face tells me she isn't buying my excuse any more than I bought the bike, but she drops the conversation as we enter the kitchen. Nick and Meg are sitting at her table gorging on homemade peach cobbler oozing with heaping scoops of vanilla ice cream.

"Hey guys, did you get your homework done?"

"Mom, you've gotta try this," Nick answers with his mouth full, and I know he hasn't opened a book.

"I did mine twice," Megan chimes in, and I don't doubt it.

While the kids bundle themselves up for the car trip home and collect their backpacks along with the remaining cobbler, Char pulls me aside.

"How about tomorrow? Should we try this again?"

She's not giving up.

"I could shop for you. Just tell me what to buy?"

The tone in her voice gives me pause: she loves my kids so much and so obviously wants them to have a good Christmas. "We'll see," I tell her, then feel ashamed by the joy my response gives her. I appreciate that she's trying to help, but I don't know if I can face another shopping disaster. Maybe *she* is the secret Santa who left the flower on the porch yesterday.

"I'll make lasagna for dinner, and we'll bake Christmas cookies while you shop. Meggie will love that."

"We'll see," I tell her again, but with firmness in my voice signaling an end to the conversation and all possibility of a repeat performance tomorrow.

"Just think about it," she says, and we both know I won't.

It is after ten p.m. when we pull into the garage at home. The house is dark, and I have no idea where Ben is, as usual. Nick and Meg empty the car of backpacks and gym bags. I send them into the house via the front door so that I can secret the remains of my binging into the trash.

"I'll be in right behind you."

Nick grabs the house key from my hand and announces his

intent to polish off the cobbler as soon as he gets inside, but Megan lingers.

"You're going to hide Christmas presents aren't you?" she asks. "Did you buy one for me?"

Her innocent question fills me with regret, and I choke on my reply, feeling as if Rick and Father Christmas have their hands clenched around my throat.

"Into the house, you. You'll find out on Christmas morning."

She skips toward the front door and is almost bowled over when Nick comes charging back into the garage.

"We got another present," he shouts, holding up two packages of Christmas bows.

The homemade card, heralding the Second Day of Christmas, gives no clue to the sender.

On the second day
of Christmas
Your true friends give to you,
Two bags of bows
for all of you.

"Wonder what we'll get tomorrow," Nick says, with a kid's confidence that more gifts will follow. "I hope we get the five golden rings like in the song."

Megan's immediate reaction is ecstasy way out of proportion to the bows themselves, which are lovely but completely ordinary.

"Momma, you can put them on our Christmas presents!"

The fudge cakes congeal in my stomach.

"We'll probably just get the bill," I answer, prodding them both into the house and slamming the door behind us. I try to remember if I had mentioned my evening plans to Joann while I was at the office, wondering if she had known that our house would be empty for a few hours so that she could deposit the gift.

The excitement over the arrival of a second gift and a sugar high from the cobbler and ice cream keeps them both awake long past bedtime. Nick is tented under a blanket playing a video game in his room, while Megan curls up in bed like a cat and asks me questions about her daddy.

"I miss him" has become her evening standard, instead of "good night."

After talking for a little while, I turn off her light and go downstairs to make up my bed on the couch. It's not long before I hear the floorboards creaking overhead. It is Megan, tiptoeing downstairs to look at the bows again.

"Who do you think is leaving the gifts?"

She opens a bag of the bows and begins to pair them up. She selects two with red and white stripes for her presents, blue for Nick, and green for Ben. I try to hide my tears, but she is a smart kid.

"Will they leave a gift tomorrow? Nick is so sure."

Unable to answer, I shrug my shoulders.

She curls up beside me on the couch and makes x's and o's on my nightgown above my heart.

"Are they leaving the gifts . . . because of Dad, because we're alone this Christmas?"

I respond with a harsher tone than I intend.

"Sometimes, adults don't have all the answers, Meg, and I

can't answer that one. I do know you'll be yawning in math class in the morning, if you don't get to bed."

"I *always* yawn in math class," she responds, not taking offense. "Besides, my science teacher says it's a kid's job to ask questions. I'm just doing my job."

"And it's my job to make sure you get plenty of rest. Now scoot."

She gives up just after midnight when I threaten to ground her from basketball practice.

"Don't forget the red-and-white bows are for my presents," her parting comment.

"I won't forget."

I listen for a few more minutes for her sock-padded shuffle coming back down the landing, but silence at last envelops the house.

The neon glow of the toggle switch on the computer offers the only sign of life in the family room. The reflection of the pulsating beam on the package of bows casts a rainbow of dancing shadows on the wall. I think maybe it's a sign. I wrap a quilt around me and sit down at the computer. My intent is to try online Christmas shopping, but the endeavor ends just as my shopping trip did. I'm in no mood for jolly, and the pair of dancing elves directing me to toys, bikes, and basketballs is beyond my level of holiday cheer. I hit the Escape key and bring up a blank page.

"Make a shopping list," I order myself. The cursor blinks and fades, twenty times, sixty, one hundred, so I flip back to a search engine and type.

"Are you there, Rick?"

My fingers hover over the Enter key, and I think how embarrassing it would be if Ben should walk in on me right now. I thump on the key anyway.

An ad flashes across the monitor: "You can find everything on eBay." Frustrated, I toss the bags of bows in the trash. The image of Megan's hopeful smile delivers a flying forehand smash to my gut. I go to bed before I have a chance to change my mind.

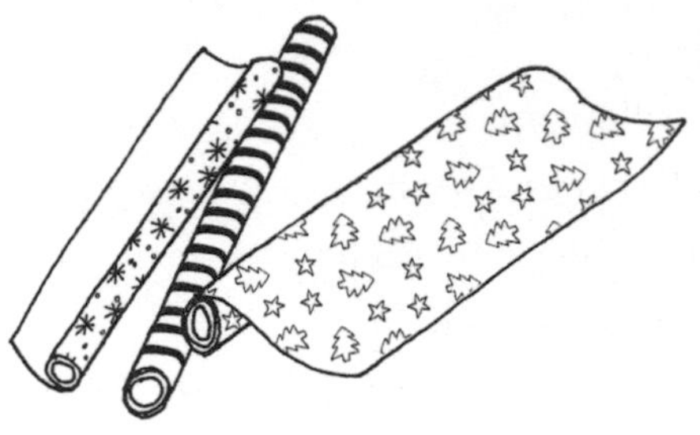

Chapter Three
The Third Day of Christmas

The Christmas bows from our true friends rematerialize the next morning, shifting from the trash can in the laundry room onto Megan's nightstand.

When my daughter finishes her cereal, I run my fingers through her hair, working out the tangles, a morning ritual we both enjoy. She closes her eyes and leans back into her seat, cascading her hair over the back of the chair.

"Sleepy?" I ask.

"Just thinking," she replies.

Ben joins us. I know that I can't let another missed curfew pass without comment. I plan my attack while he heats instant oatmeal in the microwave. I let him take a few bites before charging.

"I didn't fall asleep until after midnight. What time did you get home?"

"Way before that," he says. "You were in the bathroom. I went straight to bed."

I want to believe him.

Megan rolls her eyes but doesn't challenge her brother. Even a little bit of rebellion is out of character for her, and I fear something is brewing between them.

Ben has one very loud word for his little sister, "What?"

"Nothing. Nothing at all," she says.

Nick wanders into the dining room playing his Game Boy. He eats dry cereal out of the box so he doesn't miss a minute of playing time. He is unaware of the tension at the table but defuses it anyway.

"We got a second gift last night," he tells his brother. "Two bags of bows."

"Where are they? Did you see who left them?"

Megan flashes me what I think is a disappointed look.

"The Christmas bows are in my bedroom," she says. "Mom doesn't want them."

The boys speak simultaneously, "Why not?"

I walk out of the room in search of my purse to avoid answering the question. Megan responds loud enough for me to hear.

"She's getting a cold."

"Another one?" Nick asks.

I pull ten dollars from my wallet and hand it to Ben, moving the conversation away from the gifts and onto dinner plans for the evening. I have a late meeting to cover for the newspaper and won't be home in time to cook. The honor falls to him.

"Can you go to the grocery after school? We need milk and butter."

I wait for Ben to erupt, but he just pockets the cash.

"There's a box of macaroni and cheese on the counter."

Megan gives Nick a pleading look, and I'm not sure what it means, but her brother's attention is tethered to Super Mario.

"I can walk to Dot's Market after school," she volunteers. "I'll get the groceries."

"How about, *no*," Ben says.

Since the market is more than a mile away, I agree with my son.

"Why don't you take your sister with you," I suggest.

The look on Ben's face is far from filial. My mom radar starts beeping when Megan melts back into her chair and closes her eyes again, but I attribute the mood to her late bedtime and my trashing of the bows.

I know what's going on. Instead of fanning her joyous spirit, I am stomping it out. I want to make amends, maybe take her to a movie this weekend.

"How about we—" The arrival of Ben's school bus outside the house ends the conversation and sends everyone scrambling. Nick's and Meg's buses are never far behind. As Ben walks out the door, I ask him to spend time with his sister this evening.

"She's ten. She doesn't need a babysitter," he says.

Though she isn't her usual chatty self, Megan gives me a long hug before she walks out to wait for her bus. The hug is reassuring and makes me feel a little better about the bows.

All three kids make it to the stop before their buses leave without them. I congratulate myself with a Diet Coke and hope the caffeine will inspire me to whittle away at the heap of dirty clothes in the laundry room. While throwing used dryer sheets into the trash, I discover Megan didn't rescue all the bows this morning. The ones made of red-and-white striped ribbon—the two she selected for herself—lie in the bottom of the bin. My heart melts, and I know with certainty that I am the worst mother in the world.

"She's losing Christmas."

Instead of piddling around home until noon getting the Smith house in shape for Christmas as planned, I arrive at the office just after ten. I tell myself this is where I need to be right now. I am building a career to support my family, but that is only partly true. I spend more time in the office than at home. It's just easier.

By the time I get back home, it is around seven p.m. I walk in the door regretting having gone into work so early. The extra hours at the office resulted in an additional story to write. I am tired. My feet hurt. Nick and Megan are sitting at the table with bowls of mac 'n' cheese before them. Ben is not around, but his car is in the driveway, and I am encouraged to see that food is on the table.

"Smells yummy."

The kids look at each other and freeze. I get no hello, or "how was your day?" The sense of relief I experienced walking through the door evaporates. I dump my coat and purse on the couch and sit down with Nick and Megan. Upon closer examination, the concoction in front of them looks like steaming bowls of cellulite. Nick's dinner is smothered in Frank's Red Hot sauce. Megan's is garnished with more dill pickles than a McDonald's uses in a day.

"It's not horrible," Nick says feebly.

"Where's your brother?"

"Basement."

In the kitchen I find the source of the cellulite. An empty jar of mayonnaise sits on the counter. There is no butter or milk in the refrigerator. I stomp off to talk to my eldest.

I had promised Ben at his father's funeral that I would not allow this death to force him into adulthood. I think that was the last time my son really listened to me. I try talking to him, but he is so angry—with me, his dad, life. His rage fuels mine, and we both explode with hurtful words and creep away exhausted by the effort. I don't fear my son, but I fear what we will say to each other at moments when the truth of our family's loss hits us broadside. When I hug him, he shirks me off. When I tread gently, he ignores me. When I yell, he yells back. I fear lightning will strike. Contemplating when it will happen or where keeps me on high alert and on edge.

I can still hear the kids talking upstairs, and their conversation confirms there is a problem.

"I hate this," Megan says to Nick.

"It's not that bad."

"Not just the food, everything. We used to talk at dinner, about school and sports and stuff. I miss Mom's roast beef sandwiches, and chicken and noodles."

"Tacos with black olives," Nick adds to the list.

Family meals used to be special. The television got turned off. Telephone calls went unanswered. Each of us shared the best of our day and the worst. Now dinners consist of cold-meat sandwiches, salads, hamburgers from a bag, and apparently mac 'n' cheese made out of mayo. There is very little conversation without Rick to lead it.

"Tell me about your day, princess." Nick gives his best impression of their dad. "How about you twirl some macaroni on that fork for me."

Of Italian descent, their father had given his fine-art-of-eating-pasta demonstration every time spaghetti appeared on the menu. Megan's utensil scrapes against her bowl, and I imagine my children attempting to spin the mac 'n' cheese around it, even though the elbow noodles aren't twirling material.

"No cutting spaghetti noodles in our house," Nick continues his dad impersonation.

The sound of Megan's laughter weighs me down, and I pause. I want to go upstairs and share these memories with my children. I want to march downstairs and get Ben to fess up about the dinner, but my body is stone. I can't move. I just lie down on the couch and listen.

"I don't want to forget Daddy's way of twirling spaghetti on a fork," Megan says softly.

Her comment quiets Nick. The two remain silent for the rest of the meal, which doesn't take long. The garbage disposal runs a long time and I suspect neither of them ate much. The aroma of pulverizing dill pickles wafts all the way to the family room.

"It's your turn to do dishes," Nick's parting comment, before his footsteps thump up the stairs to his room.

"Why is it always my turn?" his sister calls after him.

A few minutes later, Megan is kneeling on the floor in front of the couch and prying open my right eyelid. She is holding the poinsettia.

"You asleep?"

"Not anymore."

"Our flower is sick."

"It just needs water. Get a measuring cup from the cupboard. Give it a quarter cup."

She talks to the plant as she walks back to the kitchen.

"You're going to be just fine," she says. Then, "Please live, little flower."

With dinner chores and homework done, Megan joins me in the family room, settling into a beanbag chair to watch television. Keeping my eyes closed, I pretend to sleep. I don't want to answer any more Christmas questions tonight, but my little chatterbox has clearly made her mental list and is checking it twice.

"Do you work late tomorrow?" she asks.

"Argh."

My groan sounds more like a huff, and I am sure Megan feels like one of the Three Little Pigs facing the Big Bad Wolf. Her home is made of straw and sticks.

"I'm sorry, Momma. I'll be quiet."

Quiet. That's what I long for, but I can't ignore the hurt look on her face.

"What's up?"

"I was just wondering . . . about getting a tree?"

I definitely saw that one coming, and I have a response prepared.

"Made any progress on your bedroom?"

Hurricane Megan has been blowing with gale force this week, depositing school clothes, sports equipment, candy wrappers, and water bottles in every nook of her room, except where they belong.

I have used her messy room and the overall disheveled condition of the house as an excuse to put off all kinds of things, and the latest is the purchase of a Christmas tree.

"If only I could get my stupid brothers to help," she says. "Can't you make them?"

"I have asked them, just like I asked you."

The conversation doesn't inspire Megan to get busy, but it does quiet her.

She channel surfs, finding news about a car accident, a robbery, and a standoff with police, instead of the holiday show or cartoon I know she prefers. When her movements morph from restless to quiet, I glance over. Though the overhead light hums, the darkness outside has crept indoors with the sunset casting shadows in corners. The late night and early rising have caught up with my Megan. Her chest slowly rises and falls in time with her slumbering breath, but her hands are clasped over her eyes. I roll into the couch, doing the same thing.

But before I can drift off, I hear the crash of shattering glass in the kitchen, and I'm pretty certain the mayonnaise jar now rests in pieces in the bottom of the recycling bin. Ben is destroying the evidence.

I have to talk to him.

When he comes downstairs a few minutes later, neither of us says a word. We are gunslingers standing twenty paces apart. We don't draw our weapons because Megan is asleep on the floor, but Ben knows that I know he never went to the grocery.

Megan's gentle snores divert our attention. Our showdown will come, but not tonight.

"Can't spend time with her if she's asleep," Ben says, covering his kid sister with a blanket.

The bravado of his words doesn't camouflage the gentleness of his actions as he tucks the blanket around his sister's toes. Ben turns off the light and the television as I request. But the door to the basement bangs behind him as he goes downstairs, and the sound jolts Megan from sleep. She is confused.

"Daddy?" she calls out.

I have heard her sleepy voice whisper his name many times in the early morning hours, as her daddy left for work. Megan's bedroom was always his last stop before heading out the door. Prone to kicking off her blankets at night, Rick never left home without tucking in his princess. Though sentimental and sweet, his actions often woke Megan. She would skitter to the window and wave good-bye as he backed out of the driveway. Of course, the wave was followed by a trip into my bed and an early wake-up for me. When I asked Rick to be quieter in the morning, he refused.

"Seeing her at the window waving reminds me why I go to work every day."

Megan sits up, and I can see from her expression that reality is returning.

Daddy's truck is not pulling out of the driveway.

My mind shouts, "Momma is here. I love you," but the words change as they spill from my lips.

"Hey, sleepy head," I say, flabbergasted at my own speech. "How about using some of that Christmas spirit to clean your bedroom."

Megan stares at me for a moment and then heads upstairs.

The room closes in around me without her. Family photos—my grandmother, mom, all the matriarchs of my family—glare down at me from the walls.

A family room is no place to be alone.

After a very few minutes, I follow Meg upstairs.

She sits with her back to the open door surrounded by sheets of construction paper. I see Ben's name printed on one with artwork cut from a CD cover glued in the center. A hand-drawn angel flies across the sheet bearing my name. Nick's holds a newspaper Nintendo ad. Each is embellished with a bow.

Christmas presents.

Megan is gathering up her art and hiding the homemade cards behind her bed before she begins organizing her stuffed animal collection.

"I just wanted to hug her," Megan confides to a plush puppy, before launching it into her toy chest.

"Just because I'm a kid doesn't mean I don't understand," she speaks this time to a photo of her dad gazing down at his newborn daughter. "How can I help, if Mom won't talk to me?"

A teacher had told Megan the family would heal, that we would all feel better, that "it just takes time." The thought seems to comfort Megan, but I don't know if I believe it. The mood in the house is getting worse as the holidays approach.

I lean back against the hall wall, ashamed to be listening, but I don't walk away.

"It's the gifts, I know nobody else wants them," Megan continues. "I'm the only one who wants Christmas."

When I hear her open a window, I think it time to intervene, until she starts talking to our true friends.

"Thank you, but please stop," she says, and I can picture her leaning on her windowsill facing the dark night. "You are making Momma sad."

I back down the hallway avoiding the floorboards that creak.

Twenty minutes later I find her still at her window, bundled in sweatshirt and mittens, listening for passing cars. I tell her to close the window, but she begs to leave it open a little longer.

"I'm listening for the gift givers," she explains. "I'm going to catch them tonight."

The furnace is roaring, and I envision the electric meter on the back of the house spinning dollar signs. But I have told my daughter no too many times these last few days.

"Ten more minutes. Then close the window. And you can clean your room while you listen."

Megan gathers an armful of her dirty clothes and deposits it in the laundry room, then ventures down to Ben's hideaway, perhaps to ask him for help with the cleaning. When she opens the door to his room, I hear the volume on her brother's stereo shoot up.

Megan doesn't tell me what he said, but she comes back upstairs shortly. Out of Ben's earshot, I hear her mutter a name for her brother that makes me smile to myself.

"Poopy head."

Nick at least listens to her idea. He agrees to clean his room but will do so using one hand while the other, and his attention, are focusing on a video game.

"You'll never get it get done that way," she complains. "Don't you want a Christmas tree?"

Nick doesn't immediately respond. When he does give her an answer, I think it is an honest one.

"I'm not sure we should get a tree," he says slowly. "I don't want Christmas. I want . . ."

He doesn't finish the sentence, and Megan heads back to her room with a resigned sigh.

Her sense of defeat doesn't last long.

Within minutes she is tossing laundry out into the hall using her best foul shot form.

"She shoots. She scores. The crowd goes wild."

A pair of blue jeans flies through the imaginary hoop, then gym shorts and basketball socks.

"She scores again. Aaaaaah."

Megan's room is starting to look much better, although I notice that she is shoving an assortment of broken toys and outgrown clothes under her bed. I'm about to suggest that we sort through some of the debris together when a car drives by with the radio blaring.

Grandma got run over by a reindeer . . .

"It's got to be them!"

She runs from her bedroom, leaps down the steps, and throws open the front door. The words of the song and the car are fading down the street.

There is no gift on the porch.

"Phooey," she says, but she is singing as she closes the door. When she realizes I am listening, though, her carol ends. I turn off the radio whenever a holiday song comes on, even though I know she cherishes the melodies. Now I'm teaching her to tune out Christmas, too.

Embarrassed at the example I am setting, I force myself to get off my butt. I might not be able to sing with my daughter right now, but I can drag a mop around the floor.

Megan is overjoyed at my activity.

"Christmas cleaning!" she says gleefully. "Thank you, Mom!"

She runs upstairs, giving me a glimmer of optimism for the outcome of her cleaning efforts. When I join her later, she is perching on a throne of pillows under the window, admiring the Christmas lights on the house across the street. The display reminds both of us of the giant Christmas tree Rick built a few years ago with similar white chasers.

"Ours covered the entire side of the house," Megan remembers. "I helped Daddy draw up the plans."

On a sunny January afternoon, she had held the ladder as her dad climbed up to take down the thirteen strands of lights. When the pair came inside, red-nosed and weary, two hours later, I made them cups of hot chocolate. They were already strategizing our light display for the following year.

"I think we dipped chocolate chip cookies in our cocoa," Megan says.

Megan's stomach growls, and I ask her about the dinner. She doesn't tattle on her older brother. I admire her loyalty but realize that I need to give Ben more oversight and less responsibility for his siblings.

"You didn't eat much?"

She shrugs.

"Want a snack?"

"Yeah!"

Megan and I go into the kitchen and I search the pantry, the freezer, the fridge for something healthy. My foraged finds are limited to a bag of stale potato chips, a brown banana, and chocolate ice cream topped with frosty-white freezer burn. I need to go to the grocery, but it's after eight p.m., and my children are hungry.

"Who wants a hamburger," I shout loud enough for all my kids to hear.

Nick's bedroom door flies open.

Megan hollers, "Wahoo."

Ben makes it upstairs faster than I have seen him move in months.

"One box of mac 'n' cheese isn't enough for all of us," he says mildly, but the kids are so pumped up about the late dinner that I don't want to ruin the mood by accusing him of neglecting his younger siblings.

As I walk to the car, Megan shouts something at me from the doorway.

"Don't forget about my school party," she hollers.

I make the gas station my first stop. There I purchase the best-looking box of cheap chocolates on the shelf for Megan's teacher. Though I'm not sure exactly when the party is scheduled, I want to buy the gift before I forget. I'll have to track down some wrapping paper, but at least we already have bows, thanks to the gift givers.

I pick up a sack of hamburgers and fries for my family, and head for home. By the time I pull into the driveway, I'm feeling pretty puffed up about my parenting skills. My kids will have a somewhat decent dinner this evening, and I've remembered to buy the Christmas gift for Meg's teacher.

"You can do this single-parenting thing," I tell myself, and in the moment I almost believe it.

While I am out picking up dinner for my kids, the third gift arrives. Megan, who was watching for my return, saw the car pull up.

"At first I thought it might be a neighbor or one of Ben's friends," she reports excitedly, as we devour cheeseburgers on the family room couch. "I was kneeling low and peeking over the sill to see what they would do next."

She didn't follow through with her plan to stop the gift giving; she didn't even race to the door to confront them. Instead, she snuck over to the door, crouching low, trying to hide, and wishing we hadn't left so many lights on downstairs so that she could get a better look at our Christmas elves.

She didn't open the door until after the purr of the car engine moved up the street. She found three rolls of Christmas wrapping paper on the porch, along with the usual note.

On the third day of Christmas
Your true friends give to you,
three rolls of gift wrap for all of you.

"I had my ear to the door," Megan says, building suspense. "I could hear the rustle of a package, footsteps. My hand was on the doorknob."

"Why didn't you open it?" Nick asks.

"Why didn't you talk to them?" Ben wants to know.

Megan surprises us when she announces that she did.

"I whispered Merry Christmas," she says. "And, thank you."

Nick thinks it a good idea she didn't open the door.

"Might stop if we spoil their fun. Maybe they'll bring us real presents on Christmas, a new television or bikes."

"These are real presents," Megan insists.

"Maybe we should start getting ready for bedtime," I declare.

The boys take off, but my daughter stays. Bella plops down next to Megan and rubs a wet nose against her hand, an invitation to scratch her neck. The child obliges, giving comfort to the one creature in the house that allows her to do so.

"Christmas is harder than it used to be," she tells the dog.

I couldn't agree more, but keep my opinion to myself. I remind Megan not to open the door if she doesn't know who is standing on the other side of it. I don't like the idea of strangers skulking around the house when I'm not home, although I am begrudgingly grateful that I don't have to make an extra stop to get Christmas wrapping paper now for Megan's teacher's gift.

"They're not strangers," Megan says. "They're our true friends."

Identifying the culprits moves to the top of my Christmas list.

Chapter Four

The Fourth Day of Christmas

I rise early to wrap the chocolates for Megan's teacher before waking the kids, but the task turns into a scavenger hunt. I search the family room and the kitchen for the wrapping paper that Megan reported receiving, finding only one depleted cardboard roll in a trash bag outside my daughter's bedroom door. I am tiptoeing across Megan's room to check her favorite stowaway spot behind the bed when a frustrated growl startles us both. Megan opens her eyes, smiles at me, and drifts back to sleep, while I track the source of the disturbance.

Nick stands at his bedroom door, kicking at a pile of dirty laundry that prevents him from closing it. I wish I could blame the mess on Meg, but the fault is mine. I had wedged the door open with the clothes after he fell asleep. Nick and I have been playing tug-of-war with that door every night for more than a month. Nick had closed his bedroom door before going to bed. Later, when I no longer heard the jingle of his video-game music, I had reopened it. It's a habit with me these days. I fear the kids will need me and I won't hear them.

"Why won't you keep the door closed?" Nick demands.

His voice trembles, and his eyes blaze with a level of anger I have never seen in my typically even-tempered son.

"I'm twelve years old. I need privacy."

"I do respect your privacy, Nick, but you don't need privacy while you're sleeping."

I wrap an arm around my son's shoulders and walk him back to bed. In the darkened room, I don't see the roll of gift wrap he left on the floor, and I trip over it. Nick picks it up and begins bouncing the roll against the bed frame, lightly at first and then harder and faster like an airplane engine revving for flight. I don't know where he's going with this, so I grab the roll and give him a gentle shove to make room for me to sit down next to him.

He leans against me. When he speaks, I understand it's not anger that he is feeling. It's anguish.

"Every time we get one of these gifts, it reminds me that Dad put off surgery to be home, with us, Christmas break."

Instead of uttering words of maternal wisdom or even comfort, I say, "Me, too."

We sit in silence until a sleepy-eyed Megan appears in the doorway yawning. She is dressed in oversized pajamas covered in dancing penguins, and most of her hair hangs in clumps in front of her face. Nick and I can't help but smile.

"You guys okay?" she asks in a guidance-counselor-like voice.

"We're good," I answer.

"My work is done here," she says, honoring us with a royal curtsey and wave. "Carry on."

Megan grabs the gift wrap from my hand before departing.

"I've been looking for this," she says, but I'm not about to let that roll disappear again.

"I've been looking for it, too. I need that paper to wrap your teacher's gift."

She extends the roll toward me and then pulls it back.

"I just need a little bit," she says. "I have presents for you guys and they need wrapping right away. Besides, I don't need to take in the chocolates until tomorrow."

"Don't use it all," I say, but she is already out the door.

Nick and I look at each other and sigh.

"There is no escaping this Christmas," he says to me in a voice so world-weary that it makes me wrap my arm around his shoulder.

Megan's antics have lightened Nick's mood for a moment, but I know the well of his sorrow runs pretty damn deep. For him, the approach of Christmas and the mysterious gifts have become a battering ram. The poinsettia, the bows, the gift wrap—each is pounding at his protective walls.

"Are you okay?" I ask.

Seconds creep by and Nick doesn't answer; he's staring at me. I don't want to be the adult in the room, the parent, the mom, but I know it's my job, so I ask him again.

"*Are* you okay?"

He answers, "No."

And his walls fall down.

"I saw everything that morning," he says. "My bedroom door was open. I saw you shake Dad, pound on his chest. I didn't want to watch, but I couldn't stop."

I had thought Nick's insistence on closing his door was just a natural rite of passage, or that he didn't want me to catch him playing video games after bedtime. This revelation is a smack-down.

"I feel like I'm stuck, Mom. Stuck in the loop of a roller coaster. I'm spinning and spinning, always stopping in the same spot . . . the morning Dad died," Nick says. "Most nights I can't sleep. When I do, I dream you are crying, and Dad's feet are sticking out from under the covers."

I can't think. I can't speak. I am back in that morning, just like Nick, until his next words lurch me forward to the present.

"I could have saved him."

Nick's statement bites at the numbness surrounding my heart, leaving a prickly sort of pins-and-needles pain. Awakening at last to my child's deep heartache, I grab Nick's chin and force him to look at me.

"You are not to blame."

Nick swats away my hand and lies down.

"He told me about the surgery. He said not to worry. He lied to me, Mom."

It's an unfair accusation and Nick needs to understand that.

"He was trying to protect you."

Nick tells me he imagines that conversation with his dad ending differently, with him insisting that his father not delay the surgery.

"I should have told him it didn't matter if he was home during the holidays. We could have spent time together every day after school. He might still be alive if I had," Nick says. "I would give anything for a do-over, anything."

Across the room on a shelf, Nick's alarm clock buzzes. Instead of getting up and turning it off, he launches a pillow toward the noise, knocking the clock to the floor. It keeps buzzing.

Ben walks past the room on the way to the shower and hollers, "Can't one of you turn that off?"

I begin the day wearier than when I went to bed, and I have the feeling my son does, too. I have to be at work by nine. I have to rescue my son from an out-of-control roller coaster. I offer Nick the same solution that I've been using to help myself.

"How about you camp out in the family room with me tonight?"

We might be avoiding this floor of the house, but at least it will bring us closer together.

"I'll blow up the air mattress," he replies.

"Letters to Santa? You want a story about a third-grade writing assignment? I have a dozen better ideas."

"Lighten up, Jo. Kids and Christmas sell newspapers," my editor says. "People want to read about more than school budgets this time of year."

I argue with him, but he is set on the premise, describing how teachers keep students focused on learning amid seasonal distractions. According to my kids, teachers have already closed books, cleared desks, and given in to holiday hoopla.

"Most schools close for winter break tomorrow."

"Great. That gives you all day today to write the story," he says.

My persuasion skills evidently need work. My editor is already adding the feature article to the budget for tomorrow's edition. No getting out of it.

I call a dozen schools and begrudgingly begin writing about ways teachers channel holiday cheer into English and math lessons. I can't help but hope for a bank robbery, or a sudden snowstorm, to preempt the article.

During my lunch hour, I keep a promise to myself and begin my search for the identity of the gift givers. I decide to draw up a list of suspects, but find I don't actually have anyone to put on it.

My coworker Joann had been my prime candidate the day the poinsettia arrived. But she flew home to Philadelphia for the holidays the day before, meaning that she wasn't even in Ohio when the gift wrap arrived at the house last night. I consider whether she might have brought on an accomplice to finish the tasks, but that sounds like an awful lot of trouble to go to just to keep a holiday secret.

I decide to call Megan's Girl Scout leader, Maribeth. She and the other moms in Megan's Scout troop cooked meals for our family three times a week for more than a month after Rick died. Creamy casseroles of chicken and broccoli, pots of chili and homemade stews showed up on our doorstep every couple of days. Unlike these mysterious Christmas gifts, the meals always came with a card signed with a real name. Maribeth had helped coordinate the effort, so perhaps she has decided to organize a holiday-gift delivery for us, too. She knows my work schedule better than most, and her family lives close, so dropping off the gifts without detection would be less complicated for her than someone who doesn't know us as well. She shuttles our daughters to Scout meetings and basketball practices. She has been a lifesaver when I get stuck at the office and Megan needs a ride.

After Maribeth and I exchange pleasantries, I get right down to business.

"There's something else I want to talk with you about, a mystery actually."

"You've got my attention."

"We've been getting gifts, Maribeth, Christmasy presents that someone has been leaving at the house the last few nights. We don't know who they're from."

I tell her about the homemade cards and describe each gift. If she is responsible for them, her reaction doesn't give it away.

"Meg mentioned the poinsettia at Girl Scouts. Who do you think it's from?"

"I thought maybe you."

She laughs.

"Guess again. Wasn't me, but I like the idea!"

"Have you heard anything, any talk maybe at school?"

"If someone from Bellbrook is behind this, they're keeping it quiet. I haven't heard anything, except from Meg and now you."

I hear a crash over the telephone line. I think it's her dog.

"Gotta go. Let me know if you find out who's sending them. What a fun thought!"

My research is cut short by a return call from a principal whose students are collecting canned goods and cash for needy families.

"We're trying to teach kids to look at giving instead of just receiving," she tells me. "One of our students felt so good about giving that she donated a piggy bank full of pennies she has been saving."

"Did you ask the families if they want your help?" I ask the principal.

I immediately regret the question.

I know the proverb, better to give than receive, but I wonder how often the receiver feels like my family—bamboozled by unwanted acts of kindness. We're just supposed to be grateful. I'm supposed to be grateful.

"Excuse me?"

I end the interview quickly and think about cutting her quotes out of the story, but I leave a few lines. For the first time, since October 8, I want to finish my work and get home. I want to be there if another gift arrives.

I make a final call before leaving the office. Charlotte picks up the receiver after the first ring and starts talking immediately.

"Did you get the bike? How about a tree? Have you started decorating the house?"

The answer is negative on all questions, so I ignore them.

"We got another anonymous gift. It came when I wasn't home, and Meg heard them come up to the front door. I'm worried."

"I can't imagine they mean you harm."

"Everyone's upset. Nick is having nightmares."

Charlotte pauses, and then says gently, "It's not the gifts they're upset about, Jo."

I can't argue with that.

❄

Hoping to make up for last night's meal, I stop at the grocery on the way home. Four teenagers wielding trumpets, a trombone, and a clarinet stand in front of the store playing "O Christmas Tree," while another hits shoppers up for donations. A poster board leaning against a stack of rock salt indicates they're collecting funds for a local family in need. The poster is embellished with hand-drawn sprigs of holly, similar to the one on our first anonymous note. I recognize the band members as classmates of Ben's, but I don't know them personally. I dig through my change purse for a donation, wondering if the offering will be used to buy additional secret gifts for my family.

I drop a few coins and what I worry might actually be two Tums into the slot at the top of the collection bucket and walk into the store.

I draw out my shopping experience in the hopes the teens will be finished with their good deed by the time I'm done. I'm relieved to see they are gone when I exit, but I can't catch a break today. There are Cub Scouts circling the parking lot like little blue vultures.

"Have you bought a Christmas tree yet, lady?"

I want to tell the kid it's none of his business, but his scoutmaster is watching. So I hand the boy a five dollar donation, load my groceries into the trunk of the car, and drive home.

When I arrive, the garage door is open, the overhead light is on, and our Christmas tree stand is sitting in my parking space. I let the car idle in the driveway thinking I should go move the tree stand. No doubt Megan is responsible for its strategic placement.

I shift the car into gear, put my foot on the gas, and I run over the metal tree stand, back up, and drive over it again.

Nick was right. I can't escape Christmas, but I can roll right past it with a V-6 engine and a good set of tires.

The emotional high I get from my act of defiance fades as I begin thinking how to explain the homicide of the tree stand to Megan. Like everything else, I add it to my list of problems to figure out. I don't even bother to hide the evidence this time. I leave the smashed stand on the garage floor under the car.

My daughter is over the moon when I walk into the house carrying four bags of groceries, and she insists on helping me cook dinner.

"Did you remember the stuff for my school party?"

"Already got it," I say, thinking of the candy I bought last night for her teacher.

"Where are your brothers?"

"Ben said to tell you he's at Robert's and to remind you he stayed home last night. Nick is watching TV."

Before we start cooking, I go downstairs to check on Nick. His air mattress is out of the box, inflated, and occupied.

"He's been lying there since we got home from school," Megan tattles. "I've been trying to get him to go through Christmas decorations with me."

I put my foot on the edge of his mattress, creating a ripple of airwaves.

"Ready for bed?"

I gather several blankets from the laundry room and toss them to my son.

"It's you and me tonight, kiddo."

Dinner preparations are delayed by a telephone call from my boss. The copy desk has a question about my school story. In the middle of our conversation, I hear what sounds like two elephants racing up the family room stairs.

Our Christmas culprits must have left another gift.

Nick and Megan are tussling over the doorstep deposit, a package of four holiday gift boxes. Megan lets go of the bag without warning, and Nick flies backward onto the air mattress. The plug pops. Nick reacts with a wrestling move. He grabs Megan around the knees and she goes down. Both of them are laughing as the mattress flattens.

"Did either of you see them?"

"Almost," Meg says.

The kids explain that when they heard a car coming toward the house, they raced to the door to see if they could catch our true friends in the act. The fray on the stairwell delayed them.

"I found the present," Nick says.

"But I reached the door first. I let you open it," Megan reminds him. "Remember what you promised."

Nick makes a face at his sister, and I get the feeling he made a promise I am not going to like.

"What's up?"

"He's going to get *all* the boxes of Christmas decorations out of the closet in the basement for me," she says.

"Nick?"

He avoids answering and instead admires the artwork on the newly arrived card. The message, again, follows "The Twelve Days of Christmas" carol. Most of the writing is in red crayon, except for the words *gift boxes*, which are in blue. The first letter in each phrase is boxed on all the lines but one.

[O]n the Fourth Day
[O]f Christmas
[Y]our true friends give
to you
[F]our Gift Boxes
[T]hree Rolls of Gift Wrap
[T]wo Bags of Bows
[O]ne Poinsettia
[F]our All of you.

"Look at this, Mom. They used *f-o-u-r* instead of *f-o-r* in the last line. That's different from the other cards."

"Well, there are four of us."

"Maybe it's a clue," Nick says. "And why are these letters boxed?"

Nick grabs paper and a pencil from his backpack and copies out each of the boxed letters: *O-O-Y-F-T-T-O-F.*

"That's not one of my spelling words," Meg says.

We try reversing the letters: *F-O-T-T-F-Y-O-O.*

"Hopeless," she says. "Maybe the boxes are for decoration."

Nick isn't giving up.

"What if there are clues on all the cards that we have to piece together."

I think he might be onto something.

"I have the first note. I'm not sure about days two and three."

"We'll save them from now on and check them every night," he says. "I'll figure this out."

A half hour ago he was ready for bed; now he's heading downstairs with his sister to unleash Christmas on the house. I'm relieved he's feeling energized by the mystery.

I go upstairs to change out of my work clothes and then check my e-mail. By the time I return to the kitchen, Megan has abandoned her brother, who says he doesn't need her help until the boxes are out of the closet.

"He didn't want me down there. Besides, I promised to help make dinner."

She lines up the contents of the grocery bags on the kitchen counter, which include the ingredients for my chicken and noodles, tacos with black olives, and spaghetti.

"How did you know?"

Panic replaces her smile when she realizes I overheard her discussion with Nick last night, then defiance.

"I'm not sorry for what I said."

"You shouldn't be." I give her a hug, and then I ask, "What do you want for dinner?"

I expect spaghetti to be her choice, but she surprises me.

"Tacos with black olives."

We brown a pound of hamburger, add the taco seasoning, and let it simmer. She opens a can of olives while I chop tomatoes and lettuce.

The aroma brings Nick out of the basement.

"Tacos, my favorite."

Megan looks at me with a smug smile.

"Again, my work is done here," she says.

Nick nips a spoonful of hot taco meat from the pan and then offers to help set the table. This is a first. I wonder if something about our conversation this morning has left him feeling more generous.

The beams from Ben's headlights flash across the living room as he pulls into the driveway, and we add a fourth plate to the table. Ben walks in wearing his dad's old work coat—faded, frayed, and way too big. The arms of the coat hang over his knuckles, and the garment could easily wrap around him twice. He's clutching the jacket closed, and I'm pretty certain he's hiding something underneath.

"Hungry?" I ask, hoping he will take off the jacket and reveal a textbook or notebook hiding in the interior pocket. He goes directly downstairs.

"Gotta wash my hands first."

Ben returns to the kitchen a few minutes later, minus the coat.

"What have you been up to?" I ask.

"Hanging out at Robert's. Nothing fun. We had math homework."

At that moment I decide to do something I swore I would never do to one of my kids. After Ben leaves for school tomorrow, I'm going to search his bedroom. I hate the idea of violating my son's privacy, but he hardly talks to me. Now, he's sneaking things into the house. I am afraid for him.

During dinner, Megan goes into detail for Ben about the arrival of the fourth gift, and Nick shares his theory about the card clues. Remembering the young musicians at the store, I ask Ben if he has many friends in the high school marching band.

"Brett plays clarinet. Why?"

I mention the band members I saw at the grocery store but don't divulge my suspicion that they could be involved with the gifts. If they are doing this for Ben, maybe they think it will help him. Maybe it will bring the old Ben back, the boy who loved being part of this family and who loved me.

While my mind is wandering, Megan is making plans for the gift boxes.

"I think we should each get one to put under the tree for each other."

Nick has no interest, but Ben—to my shock—walks off with one.

Nick lingers to help me with the kitchen cleanup. When he rolls up his sleeves and washes the dishes, I know that something is afoot, but I decide not to worry about it tonight. For the second day in a row, the kids and I have dined together. This evening I even prepared a home-cooked meal. The house is far from clean, but it's also not a mess, and I have a plan to deal with Ben. As I lie down to sleep later that night, with Nick slumbering on an air mattress a few feet away, I feel hopeful this fog of grief we've been lost in is lifting just a little.

Chapter Five

The Fifth Day of Christmas

I drag myself from the couch when the alarm clock buzzes at five thirty a.m. instead of hitting the snooze button, like usual. There will be no arguments over who takes the first shower this morning. As I get ready for the day, I go over my to-do list. The kitchen is stocked with enough food to create a breakfast buffet, and I personally plan to make sure no one misses the school bus.

After the success of last night's dinner and the arrival of a fourth anonymous gift, I commit to becoming a more fully functional mom, and this morning is the launch of the new me. Just as I am pumping myself up about doing this single-parent thing, Megan knocks on the bathroom door. I expect to see her joyful face when I open the door; instead, I see worry lines wrinkling her brow.

"I can't find the cupcakes."

"Cupcakes?"

"For the holiday party at school. You signed up to bring them at the open house. Remember, I asked you about them yesterday?"

The open house was in September.

"When's the party?"

"Today."

I've volunteered to supply a snack for Megan's holiday party every year. She and I usually cuddle over cookbooks and seasonal magazines to find an unusual treat we can bake together. We've made Christmas wreath cookies of cornflakes and melted marshmallows, and candy-cane reindeers. I have been stumbling through December trying to forget about Christmas and failing miserably. The one thing I had promised to remember, I forgot.

"The school was supposed to send a reminder."

"It's on the refrigerator. I gave it to you last week."

Megan leans against the bathroom door and gives me a frustrated look.

"Did you forget?"

The scene replays somewhere in my frontal lobe, beginning with Megan handing me the note. I had indeed promised to make the cupcakes and had just as quickly forgotten all about them.

"I remembered the gift for your teacher," I say, trying to soften my daughter's disappointment. She puts her hands over her eyes and shakes her head.

"What are we going to do?" she asks.

It's not the first time since Rick's death that I have screwed up like this; the ingredients I bought to make popcorn balls for her harvest party are still in the pantry. But it's another Christmas moment I'm denying my child, and I can't handle disappointing her again.

"We could make something quick. Popcorn?"

"You signed up on the sweet list," Meg says, looking encouraged that I am thinking of possible solutions to the snack crisis. "That means sugar."

I don't have time to bake, so I improvise.

"Finish getting ready. We're going to the store."

The trip to the grocery requires us to leave the house before the boys get on the school bus, and I'm worried Ben may use the opportunity to skip class. It also delays any chance I might have had to look around his bedroom this morning. I wrestled with the idea a good part of the night. Our relationship, though shaky right now, is built on trust. Searching his room will destroy that if he finds out, but it's got to work both ways. I saw him sneaking something into the house last night. I need to know what's going on with him.

Before Meg and I leave, I take Ben aside.

"Promise you'll get on the school bus."

Ben takes a deep breath, and I recognize the look on his face. It's the same one I give him when he pushes my patience to the limit.

"Do you really need to ask that?"

Megan steps in, "Please Ben."

"Whatever," he says. "I promise."

I am backing the car out of the driveway when Nick runs out of the house wearing his coat, pajama pants, and snow boots.

"I need to talk to you. It's important."

"Can it wait until after school?"

Nick's expression tells me it shouldn't, but when he says yes, I take him at his word.

"I don't work today. I'll be waiting when you get off the school bus."

As he walks back into the house, I notice a manila envelope in his hands, and I wonder what's inside.

Please, no more trouble. No more problems.

During our drive to the store, Megan rattles off a list of alternative treats in case the cupcakes are a no-show in the bakery aisle.

"Doughnuts with sprinkles, cookies, a giant Christmas cake, umm . . . pumpkin pie with whipped cream."

I expect the store to be deserted because it's so early, but it seems that I'm not the only parent seeking school party supplies. I'm about to call out a greeting to a pair of moms who have kids in Megan's class, when I overhear their conversation.

"She blew off the harvest party. I'm buying extra cupcakes just in case."

"I hear the family is falling apart."

I stop walking and take hold of Megan's hand so she stops, too. A blank expression replaces her smile. I'm hoping a black hole sucks us in before the ladies turn around and detect our presence, but Megan has other plans. She starts singing.

"He's making a list. Checking it twice. Going to find out who's naughty or nice."

The ladies turn to see Megan taking hold of our shopping cart and plowing down the aisle in their direction. Her legs move with propeller speed toward the cupcake display. She stops short of disaster and says, "Excuse me."

They step out of her way.

I join my girl, and we load cupcakes into our cart. She continues singing "Santa Claus Is Coming to Town," emphasizing the word *naughty*.

Her daddy and I used to sing that tune whenever one of the kids acted out when they were little. I wonder if Megan sings it now for the busybodies or for me. The women hadn't said anything that wasn't true. We are falling apart.

When the ladies move out of the aisle, I whisper to Meg, "I'm sorry. I'll do better."

She acts as if nothing happened.

"Let's get an extra half dozen in case someone wants seconds," she says instead, adding more cupcakes to our shopping cart.

I see that she is smiling again, but now there are tears welling in the corners of her eyes.

We encounter the women one more time in the checkout lane. Megan pointedly wishes them a happy Christmas. I walk out without saying a word to either of them.

Except for the hum of the car engine, the ride to school is a silent journey. Megan takes her time transferring the cupcakes from the plastic store containers into our decorative ones. She snaps down the last lid as I pull into a parking space.

"Try to have fun today," I tell her. "Don't let those ladies get to you."

To my surprise, she laughs.

"Those women don't get what we're going through, not like the gift givers," she says. "We're not falling apart; we're just chipped a little bit. You do what you can, Mom. We all do."

Megan leans across the center console of the car and gives me a kiss on the cheek before getting out.

As I watch her swaying ponytail disappear into the crowd entering the school building, I see not the ten-year-old she is, but the young lady she is becoming. My heart glows with maternal pride, and I sit there basking in it, until I notice one of the moms from the store pulling into the parking space next to mine. I am pretty sure there is an apology written on her face, but I don't want or deserve it. I back the car out as she approaches. I have nothing to say. My daughter has said it all.

I spend most of the day scrubbing floors, washing dishes, and doing lots of laundry. My kids need me to take charge, and I don't want to let them down any more than I already have. Now that Nick has removed the holiday decorations from the basement closet, I know it won't be long before ceramic Santas start appearing around the house. My goals are to make sure the decorations won't be sitting in dust clouds and that we have clean clothes to wear next week.

It feels good to do normal things, chores I have done every year to prepare for the holidays since I was a new bride. I appreciate the solitude of the house, the quietness. Instead of feeling lonely and stiff, I feel free to let my mind wander back to happier Christmases and to cry if I want to, without fear of upsetting one of the kids.

My holiday preparations always began in mid-November with a floor-to-ceiling scrub of everything in the house, a tradition of my mom's that I adopted. Our first Christmas together, Rick had volun-

teered to help before he realized how extensive the work was actually going to be.

"Nobody's going to notice if you don't vacuum under the bed," he had complained two days into our Christmas cleaning. "Who cares about dust on the top of the chandelier that can only be seen if you're seven feet tall?"

After a weekend of scrubbing floors, cleaning toilets, de-cobwebbing light fixtures, washing down walls, and polishing every wooden surface in the house, Rick labeled me "Christmas crazy." In future years to avoid participation in the cleanup, he would plan some vital home repair—like replacing the plastic vent on the dryer or changing the batteries on our seven smoke alarms—that simply had to be completed over the holidays. That was fine with me as long as he stayed out of my way. I'd flip on the radio and sing along to Christmas songs while the housework tinted my hands and knees the color of pink poinsettias.

The real Christmas fun began after the cleaning. That's when I'd drag out the decorations. A Santa figurine dressed in Pilgrim apparel standing next to a turkey, a gift from my sister Carol, was always the first holiday dressing to be displayed. For us, and then later for the kids, his appearance was a sign that a month of holiday fun was about to begin. Thanksgiving was a blur this year, and the little fellow never made it out of the cupboard.

I'm nearly to the bottom of the laundry pile—I can actually see the floor for the first time in weeks—when I unearth a cache of Rick's clothing: socks, underwear, the gray-striped shirt he wore the day before he died. The sleeves are still rolled up to the elbows, a necessity because his long arms usually stuck out of his sleeves. I gather the shirt and hold it to my nose, breathing deeply.

Mildew.

The shirt has been sitting on the laundry room floor under wet towels and dirty gym clothes. Any trace of my Rick is gone.

I dump extra laundry detergent into the washer as it fills with hot water and then collect Rick's clothing. Before I toss in the shirt, a note slips out of pocket. The paper is damp, but a list written in Rick's perfect block penmanship is legible: "Christmas gifts to buy before surgery—bike for Nick, seat covers for Ben's car, a Bellbrook warm-up suit for Meg. Nerf guns for everybody."

Under my name, he has written "This Christmas is going to be special."

I trace each letter on the page wondering when he wrote the list, and where. The empty washing machine runs through the wash cycle while I read the short missive over and over, committing it to memory. I'd like to think it's a sign from Rick that he is somehow still with us, but I know it's just another piece of his unfinished life.

I refold the note and put it back in the shirt pocket, then restart the washing machine. I stuff Rick's socks, his underwear, and the shirt into the washer, and I watch, mesmerized, as the hot water begins to rotate. I regret my action almost immediately, but not soon enough to save the note. It is in pieces, like our lives.

Vapor rising from the hot water makes me feel like I'm in a steam room, so I flip the lid closed, but it doesn't help. I am sweating, and my heart jumps and leaps like it wants out of my chest. I wonder if this is how Rick felt, and I panic. My legs buckle, and I slip to the floor.

"Breathe. Stay calm. Help me, Rick."

I fall asleep sitting there on the concrete floor, leaning against the washer.

When I wake, the house is quiet, and my heart beats normally. Only the fear remains. The house feels unwelcoming, and I don't want to be here alone. I run upstairs, slip on my snow boots, grab my car keys and coat. I have to get away.

I drive for three hours, to Cincinnati and back, without getting out of the car.

Nick opens the front door for me when I arrive home just after five o'clock. He has been home for more than an hour, but he doesn't ask me where I've been. A CD with a collection of my favorite songs is playing on the stereo. Megan, he informs me, needs a ride home from basketball practice at seven thirty; Ben is chopping firewood with a friend, and he's going to get paid.

Nick pulls off my coat by the cuffs, folds it over his right arm and motions for me to take a seat.

"Your throne, madam."

I roll my eyes with a smile as the butler act continues.

He props a pillow behind my head and then kneels before me like Prince Charming, only there are no glass slippers, just my snow boots, which he removes. A mug of tepid hot chocolate sits on the coffee table with chunks of cocoa powder floating on the surface. Next to the cup is a toasted Pop Tart, which Bella is eyeing, on my favorite holiday platter.

The dish, which Rick purchased for me several Christmases ago, only comes out of the cupboard on holidays. The triangle-shaped platter with a Christmas tree etched on it was not expensive. It's not even all that pretty, but it is special to me. Many a festive dinner was served on this platter—my traditional roasted turkey, ham smothered in maple syrup, and pork loin with sauerkraut. The gift of the platter had been Rick's validation that, while I might not be a master chef, I could put together a cheery and tasty meal for our friends and family.

Nick massages my temples.

"Sit back. Relax. Enjoy," he says.

My son's attentiveness heightens my tension, instead of relieving it. When the voice of Kenny Loggins singing "Danger Zone" starts playing on the stereo, I know it's literally time to face the music.

"What's up?"

Nick laughs, stops the massage, and helps himself to a generous bite of my Pop Tart. He hands me the envelope I saw him carrying this morning.

"I made a Christmas list."

Inside the envelope is a four-page opus that my son has divided into categories and alphabetized. The video games, music, and bike I expect to see aren't even listed.

"You want two gallons of wall paint for Christmas?"

"I *want* to move my bedroom," he says. "There's lots of space in the basement next to Ben's. It just needs a little sprucing up."

My gut reaction: no way this is happening. But I take a deep breath and decide to hear him out.

"Where'd this idea come from?"

"The gifts."

I renew my commitment to identify the gift givers so that I

can delegate to them the task of cleaning out the basement and painting the room.

"I told Megan I wouldn't help her get out the Christmas decorations," he says. "But with all the gifts and everything, I started wanting to do it. When I turned on the basement light, I knew it was perfect for me."

I'm not sure how to answer him yet, and decide to stall by looking through his Christmas list again. I start on page one. The sheet contains paint and related supplies, brushes, rollers, drop cloths. Nick also provides intel on the approximate cost and the cheapest place to buy each of the items.

I have seen a list like this before, not this exact one, but similar. Rick presented one to me before he started building shelves in the family room closet last December. I had begged him to delay the project until after the holidays, but as usual he used his charm to convince me otherwise. I'm not going to be such a softy with Nick.

The second page suggests new furnishings.

"I don't want to sleep on a waterbed anymore. It wasn't good for Dad. It's not good for me."

The next page has softer supplies: sheets, a bedspread. The final page holds "vital but Christmas-optional items" that Nick acknowledges may have to wait until his birthday in April or beyond, due to the cost.

"A computer and a television?" I say, amazed at his boldness. "How about I throw in a hot tub and mini fridge."

Nick doesn't find my comments funny.

"I'm almost a teenager," he says. "I can't function in that tiny room anymore."

Nick does have the smallest bedroom in the house, the one we used as a nursery, when we moved to Bellbrook in 1983, just before Ben celebrated his first birthday. Back then we used the basement as an exercise room housing my stationary bike, Rick's inversion boots, and some free weights. The room was poorly lit, had concrete walls lined with pink insulation, and the sole heating duct didn't warm the space.

When Nick came along, and eventually Megan, Rick and I talked about our need to finish the basement, but my husband was working fifty-five hours a week, and he wasn't motivated to take on a major remodel. When Megan turned four and I returned to Wright State University to complete my undergraduate degree, Rick wanted a project of his own. He drew up plans for a rec room for all our children and a bedroom for our eldest so he wouldn't have to share bunk beds with his kid brother. While I attended class, Rick put the kids to bed and then worked on the basement, hanging drywall, laying carpet, painting. When Ben finally moved downstairs, Nick suggested that he switch rooms with Megan to take ownership of the smallest bedroom.

Less to clean was his reasoning.

So we painted the larger bedroom cotton-candy pink and the smaller one neon lime green, colors Rick let the kids select.

Our middle child has always been our science-and-technology geek, so his dad hand-painted the constellations on Nick's bedroom ceiling using a template and glow-in-the-dark paint. The painstaking process had taken Rick weeks to complete, because he insisted the sky map be accurate and done to scale. Once the map was completed, father and son stargazed from the comfort of Nick's bed until the constellations vanished into the darkened ceiling.

"It may be the smallest room, but it's going to be special," Rick had said.

I can't imagine Nick in any other bedroom.

My brain vaults across all the reasons why the move to the

basement isn't a good idea for Nick, and I stick the landing on a big one.

"Have you mentioned this to your brother?"

Nick shakes his head reluctantly. "No."

"I didn't think so."

My two younger children have mostly ceded the basement rec room to their older brother since their dad's death, avoiding clashes with Ben and his buddies, who have claimed the space for themselves. I don't want Nick to start a territory war, but on the other hand, the proximity of their rooms could help strengthen Nick's relationship with his big brother. I am torn.

"After the first of the year, Nick. We can talk about it."

True to his nature, Nick persists.

"It's all I want for Christmas, Mom. A new room. It's all I want."

I hand him the platter, minus the toaster pastry.

"I get it, Nick. I'm not saying, no. I'm saying not right now."

Nick plops the platter on the kitchen counter, and it spins like an off-balance top. We both pounce to keep it from falling, but it slips and crashes to the floor. Nick's face is ashen as he immediately begins picking up the pieces.

"I'm sorry, Mom. I'm so sorry."

I don't hear the apology. The words of the women in the store this morning are ricocheting around in my brain: "the family is falling apart, falling apart, falling apart."

Their hurtful words intertwine with the message on Rick's note: "Christmas will be special."

The tears I've been hiding for two months come rushing out of me.

"Everything is broken. We're broken."

My outburst sends Nick fleeing to his room—his small, green, constellation-ceilinged room. I sit on the floor, picking up the pieces through blurred vision, and I cut my finger on a shard.

I sit on the floor, thinking, while I watch the blood drip from my finger onto the pieces of the plate. I woke up this morning feeling like I might be able to get through the day in one piece, yet I had let myself get derailed by the women in the grocery store. But if Megan can believe that we aren't broken, if Nick can find a way to move forward, then I can, too. Rick had wanted this Christmas to be special, and I am the one here to make his wish come true. When the blood clots, I stand, wash my hands, and then wrap a bandage around the cut.

"Do what you can," I tell myself.

The mess on the kitchen floor is a quick cleanup.

With new resolve, I head downstairs to assess the state of things. The rec room is littered with boxes, but there is a narrow path leading to Ben's basement hideaway. When I flip on the light switch, his room comes alive. The television turns on and so does the fan.

Rick's beige coat is lying on the floor next to the bed. A plastic bag from Dollar Tree sticks out of the pocket. I can't help but look inside. There is no booze. No pot. No cigarettes. The bag holds a foam ball and a kid's basketball hoop that attaches to the wall with suction cups and two comic books in a plastic sleeve.

"Christmas gifts for Nick and Megan?"

It's enough to make me cut my search short. Only my guilt leaves the room with me. For months I have been suspicious of Ben's actions, wary about his late nights, suspecting that he may land in a scrape with the law. Now, I know where the grocery money went. Could he be our Secret Santa? Or is he buying Christmas gifts for his siblings because he knows I have not.

This has been a day for lessons, and I don't like learning any of them, but in my heart I know I need to.

I spend an hour in the rec room looking for good reasons why Nick should not move down here, logical ones that he will accept without argument. There are bins of outgrown clothes and broken toys, bundles of old newspapers, and boxes holding the remains of Rick's office at Gem City Engineering: pencils, pens, family photos that used to sit on his desk. All is protected under double layers of bubble wrap.

Crates of Rick's record album collection are stacked in piles, just as he left them after he replaced our favorites with compact discs. Leo Kottke, Pink Floyd, Yes—the groups set the early years of our marriage to music. The song lists feel like old friends, and the cardboard album jackets, individual pieces of art. I start sorting through them and set several aside to share with Ben, who inherited his dad's taste in music. This room is crowded with memories that would need a new home if Nick's bedroom displaces them, but perhaps that wouldn't be the worst thing that could happen.

The doorbell rings, giving me an excuse to escape from my contemplation.

By the time I reach the living room, Nick is running up the driveway with a gift bag in his hand.

He reenters the house excited, but hesitates when he sees me. I suspect he is gauging whether my meltdown has reached nuclear magnitude, or if I've cooled off. In truth, I'm somewhere in the middle, but I smile and motion for him to have a seat beside me on the sofa.

"I didn't recognize the car," he says, slightly out of breath.

He pulls five angel note cards from the gift bag and hands them to me. He notices my bandaged finger.

"What happened?"

"It's just a little cut. I'm clumsy."

"Mom . . ."

"We're good," I tell him. "Let's see if we can find a clue on our Fifth Day of Christmas card."

We compare the new card to the earlier ones.

"This one's a lot different, simpler," Nick observes. "It doesn't look like the same person made them."

"You could be right," I agree.

There are no hand-drawn holly leaves or embellishments. The card is made of green construction paper cut with pinking shears, so the edges are zigzagged.

"The date is written at the top. That's different," Nick says. "And the words are printed, not in cursive."

The message on the card is similar to the others.

12-17-99
On the fifth day
of
Christmas . . .
your true friends
give to you . . .
5 angel note cards
4 gift boxes

3 rolls of gift wrap
2 bags of bows
&
1 poinsettia . . .
for all of you.

"Who would do this for us?" I say out loud, not really questioning Nick, but the universe.

He shrugs his shoulders.

"Santa Claus, the tooth fairy, might as well be the bogeyman for all we know," he says.

Our conversation lulls, until Nick spots the stack of albums I carried up from the basement. He folds his hands as if praying, then silently mouths the word *please*. But his face is already splitting into a big grin, and I can tell he knows he's made his case.

It feels good to see my son smile. I let the words spill out, before I have a chance to rethink them.

"We'll have to clean, gut it completely, and paint," I tell him, feeling the weight of Christmas pressing down on my chest. Now, though, I can at least appreciate the light in Nick's eyes as he realizes he might get the gift that he wants.

"You won't have to do anything," he insists. "Leave it to me."

We descend the basement steps, together this time.

Chapter Six

The Sixth Day of Christmas

I wake with aching muscles from sorting through pounds of debris in the basement the night before, but for the first time in months I feel good about all we accomplished. Nick and I had decluttered part of the rec room, taking only a short break to collect Megan from basketball practice and then to gobble some chicken wings—not most kids' idea of a great Friday night, but my kid was up for the challenge. By midnight we had filled thirteen trash bags and four boxes of clothing to donate to charity. All told, we had cleared out about a quarter of the room.

While Nick and I were sorting and organizing, Megan carried the Christmas decorations up to the family room under the ruse of getting them out of our way. By the time we went to bed, she had created a haphazard wonderland around the house. Sleighs, snowmen, Nativity scenes, and strings of white lights sparkled from every spare inch of shelf space, except in the basement.

"As soon as you're done with the painting, I'll work some Christmas magic down here," she had promised her brother before we turned in for the night.

The next morning, I'm lounging on the couch giving my muscles a break before attacking the basement once again, when Charlotte rings the doorbell and lets herself into the house. I presume she's here to talk about the success of my Christmas shopping, or to expose my utter failure at it.

"Anybody home?"

When I hear her footsteps on the stairs, I pull a blanket over my head. My sister-in-law tugs the coverlet off.

"Gracious, Jo. Do you know what time it is?

"Noonish?"

Charlotte throws up her hands.

"It's Christmas time, girl!"

She walks around the room, noting the thrown-together look of the Christmas decorations, and guesses my daughter has had more to do with their placement than me.

"You can't expect Meggie to pull Christmas off all by herself."

"I was up late working on Nick's gift," I say in self-defense.

"Did you buy the bike?"

"Not yet."

"Video games?"

"No."

"Then what did you get him?"

I share our plan to move Nick's bedroom to the basement with Charlotte, and I tell her why we need to rush the project.

"Once Nick makes up his mind, nothing changes it," she agrees. "He's like his daddy that way. Rick always got a project going right before Christmas, and as I recall, you were never happy about it."

"I'm not thrilled now, but Nick and the gift givers got the better of me."

"Did you get another gift?"

I retrieve the five angel note cards from the kitchen and show them to her.

"If you know anything about these, please tell me. Nick said the gifts *inspired* him to help Megan haul out our holiday decorations. That's when he got the idea to move his room. Honestly, these gifts are taking on a life of their own, and I'm not sure I like it."

"If these little gifts help your kids heal, what's the problem?"

I don't have an answer for her, but she has one for me.

"Help comes in all kinds of packages, Jo. Don't worry about who delivers it. Just accept."

Her words are like an instruction book written in a language I am just beginning to understand. My mind tells me all the information I need to get by is right there; I want to take it all in and believe, but I'm not ready yet.

"I don't need anyone confusing my kids. They're confused enough already. Megan is convinced we're experiencing some sort of Christmas miracle, and now this thing with Nick."

"What about Ben?"

"He still doesn't talk to me."

"Well, at least he's immune to their magic," Char says, then walks over and gives me a hug. "The holidays will pass. The gifts will stop coming, and you will figure out how to get on with your life."

I break her hold on me.

"I'm just trying to survive the next seven days."

Charlotte rearranges a Nativity scene on the bookshelf, pairing Mary with Joseph instead of with one of the three kings, and then turns to speak to me.

"Quit trying to be Wonder Woman," she says. "I'm on my way to the mall. What can I do to help?"

I'm tempted to take her up on the offer.

"Nick wants a television, a computer with a 'monster-sized monitor,' and a new bed."

Charlotte laughs.

"That sounds like our Nicky. I was thinking more along the lines of Legos," she says, marching upstairs to wake Nick and Megan. "I'll find out what they want."

I follow Char upstairs, intending to take a shower while she talks to the kids. I'm glad for a few minutes on my own. A part of me knows she is right. What harm would it do, really, if I give in to Christmas for the sake of the kids? Is it disrespectful to Rick's memory, or is it what he would have wanted me to do? I keep playing both scenarios over in my mind. I am so confused. Rick promised we'd grow old together. He left us, left me. But he is the one man who ever made me feel truly loved, besides my dad. I'm not sure if this longing I've been feeling lately to get a grip and move on is natural, or if I am somehow betraying him.

Behind the safety of the bathroom door I can hear Char talking with Nick and Megan, laughing. I sit down on the bathroom floor, and lean against the door, listening. With Char around,

I'm like a patron in a movie theater. I can be an observer, rather than a part of the action.

In our house, making a Christmas list has never been something left to the last minute. It's a process that evolves from the first snowfall to the arrival of the newspaper sale ads on the morning of December 24. Getting the good stuff involves persistence, patience, and hours of studying store catalogues and circulars. Each time a new wish book arrived at the house, the kids would crowd around me, vying to see their favorite sections.

"Doesn't anyone want to sit next to me?" their dad would tease, knowing that for the moment his parental appeal couldn't rival the slick, colored pages. Eventually, he, too, moved from the far end of the sofa to sit beside us, looking at new seasonal offerings and sale merchandise.

The ads have been recycled this year without dog-eared edges.

Nick assures Char he needs a fog machine, a black light, and glow-in-the-dark posters for his new room, all additions to the wish list he gave me. Megan says she wants one thing.

"A Christmas tree. It won't be the same if we don't get one."

The veil of sadness that began lifting last night as Nick and I worked on the basement tries to slip back down, but this time, I push it back. This holiday season won't be the same, whether or not we get a tree.

Ready or not, Christmas will come.

Twenty minutes later, I emerge from the bathroom showered and dressed. Charlotte is sitting in the living room waiting for me.

"What're you doing tonight?" she asks.

"I got nothing."

"We're getting those kids a Christmas tree, and don't you tell me no. I'll pick you up at seven. Tell Nick and Meg to dress warm. Ask Ben to come along. He can carry the tree."

My sister-in-law leaves before I can give her a reason I can't go tonight. In truth, I'm grateful she has taken the decision out of my control. And she's right. I don't want to let Megan, or any of my kids, down. With her in charge of the expedition, we'll get the tallest, fullest tree in town, and probably for less than anyone else would have paid. I wonder if I can persuade her to decorate the thing once we get it home, too.

Ben walks up from the basement just as Charlotte backs her truck out of the driveway.

"What's going on?" he asks.

Time to tell him about the bedroom switch.

"Your brother's been struggling since Dad died. He needs a change. We're cleaning out the front of the basement and turning it into a room for him."

I brace for a confrontation.

Ben sits down next to me and lays his head back on the couch. For the first time in months, he looks me in the eyes, and I see the sweet little boy who once asked Santa to bring him a sibling in his Christmas stocking.

"It's a good idea," he says finally—to my surprise. "I can't imagine what it's like sleeping up there. I don't even like going upstairs to take a shower."

While I sit mute, marveling at the fact my son is communicating with me and showing concern for his younger brother, he brings up another issue.

"What about Megan? Is she going to be all right sleeping upstairs alone?"

"She knows the plan, and she hasn't complained."

"She never does," Ben says, and I acknowledge he is right. "Maybe she and Nick should both move downstairs for a while, just a couple of months until you feel comfortable sleeping in your room again."

"You wouldn't mind having both of them downstairs?"

"I'll hate it, but I understand."

He's being so agreeable, I decide to push my luck.

"Does this mean you'll help us clean out the rec room today?"

Ben grimaces but agrees. So I pose one more question.

"Char is taking us to get a tree tonight. Come along?"

My question dams the goodwill that is flowing.

"I'll do anything for you, Mom, but not that. Leave me out of the Christmas plans."

I feel very much the way I did on Ben's fourth Christmas, when he was so excited about a gift he had made for me that he unwrapped the present himself. His eyes had glowed when he handed me the red scarf cut from the folds of my very best dress with kid scissors.

"I made it for you," he had said.

What mother can resist that kind of love?

Now he offers me this new gift, the first real expression of love he's shown since the death of his dad. But, this gift, too, cuts like the scissors on the scarf. I am worried about the anger he harbors, but relieved the angst is not directed toward me.

Yesterday, when I found the Christmas gifts he bought for his siblings, I thought maybe he had come to terms with the holidays on his own. Now, I know that he still has a way to go.

I don't press him, though; honestly, I know how he feels, and I'm glad that I can give my son a little relief from the barrage of

Christmas that I can't seem to escape. I shift our conversation back to the basement project.

We hear mumbling and turn to see Nick and Megan sitting on the steps.

"So we're going to be roomies?" Ben asks his younger brother.

"I won't get in your way," Nick says.

"I know, 'cause I won't let ya."

I end their banter with one word, "Breakfast."

I scramble a dozen eggs, and the four of us eat in the rec room surveying what needs to be done to make the space livable.

"I vote we throw out everything and start over," Ben says.

"We could sweep all this stuff into garbage bags and put them outside for the trash guys to pick up," Nick says. "We'd get done in no time."

I give Nick a "get serious" look.

"Let's put everything for Goodwill in the corner by the closet. Trash goes by the steps so we can carry it out easily," I say. "If there is anything we want to keep, we've got to find a new place for it right away or it gets pitched, too."

We spend the early afternoon sorting. My children each claim some of the items from Rick's office, which are packaged in layers of bubble wrap. Ben saves his dad's key to the executive washroom at Gem City, which is basically a rusty nail in an old wooden box, a gift from fellow toolmakers to Rick when he made the leap into management. Nick takes mechanical pencils and metal rulers. Megan grabs the family photo that had been on her daddy's desk. What's left we add to a pile of giveaways for Goodwill and a local shelter for battered women and children. We work in silence all afternoon, no music and little conversation. All of the kids take breaks to pop bubble wrap like it's some sort of therapy. Every time the room gets too quiet, the farting noises erupt for a while.

Everybody giggles, except me. I do not share in their lightness. It's been a long time since I have clowned around with my kids. I'm hoping it's like riding a bike and I will eventually get the hang of it again.

"Try it," Nick encourages me, offering me a plastic bubble to pop. "It's addictive."

"How about we throw it away?"

"I think it might be against the law to waste good bubble wrap," Nick replies, punctuating his point with a loud pop.

With all of us working, it only takes a few hours to clean out the basement. I fill buckets of soapy water to wash cobwebs off the walls and baseboards, but I leave that task to the kids.

"What color paint should I buy?"

I direct my question to Nick, but he and Ben answer together.

"Black," they say, looking like conspirators.

"Not happening. How about white?"

Ben answers, "That'll do."

I make a quick trip to the hardware store for paint. When I return, everyone has changed into old clothes, and drop cloths cover the carpet.

"Let's roll," Nick says, dipping his paint roller into the tray.

We pelt him with paint-stir sticks and rolls of blue tape.

By six o'clock, the walls glow with a fresh coat of primer. Ben, Meg, and I stop to get cleaned up. Nick finishes the trim work alone.

I am amazed at the speed of our progress today. Even more,

it feels wonderful to have everybody working together on a common goal. I whisper a prayer of thanks to the gift givers and think maybe this is how we get through Christmas. Who needs holiday hoopla, presents, and parties? We have each other. That's all we need.

The day has been so consolatory that I think about asking Ben one more time if he'll join us this evening. Megan stands at the living room window watching for her aunt Char, contemplating out loud the merits of long-needled pines. When she asks Ben his opinion, he reverts to my quiet, sullen son.

Char pulls into the driveway promptly at seven p.m., just as Ben screeches out in his red Nissan.

"Where's he going in such a hurry?" Char asks. "Isn't he coming with us?"

I shake my head. "No. He's not coming."

"Did you ask him?"

"Of course I did."

"What are we going to do with that boy?"

She's not expecting an answer, but I give her one.

"He's been helping with the basement. We've already gotten a coat of paint on the walls."

"That's progress," Char concedes. "Where's Nick?"

"I'm down here," he hollers. "Come see."

She finds Nick as white as the walls, covered in flecks of paint, looking as if he's been caught in a snowstorm.

"I wanted to paint the walls black, but Mom wouldn't let me."

"Good call," Char says with a smile. "Get your coat on, Nicky boy. We're getting a tree."

We climb into Charlotte's truck and drive to the Cub Scout

tree lot in downtown Bellbrook. I wonder if the scoutmaster will remember me. I needn't have worried.

The lot is dark, and the tree stands are nearly empty.

"There were dozens of trees here the other day," Megan says, sounding worried. "What if we can't find one?"

"We'll find one," Charlotte reassures her.

We drive into Kettering and stop in the lawn and garden center of the Meijer store. One white spruce, the only tree left on the lot, looks as if it has been leaning against a fence for weeks. The branches on one side are completely flattened.

"Not a problem," Char says. "We'll place that side against the wall. It won't take up as much space that way."

A freezing rain begins to fall. Nick and I are anxious to get out of the weather, but Megan and Char are determined to make a purchase. We march inside the store and fetch the lot attendant. He holds up the tree for us to examine and tries to shake out the smashed branches. They don't budge.

"Frozen," he says. "Give it a day or two in the house, and they'll fluff out."

"We'll take it," Charlotte says, handing the clerk a twenty dollar bill, though the price of the tree is thirty-five dollars.

"Pitiful thing. Nobody else is going to buy it," she tells the attendant. "Nick, help the young man load it into the back of the truck."

From start to finish, the tree purchase takes all of ten minutes.

"That's got to be a record," Charlotte says.

Christmas tree–hunting expeditions with Rick had been epic. He would get a tip about a reasonably priced tree lot or farm from someone at work and would start planning our trip immediately. The excursions always began early on a Sunday morning and involved packing a picnic lunch, which we ate with the heater blasting in our minivan in the early years and later in the GMC Suburban Rick's dad bought for our family.

We traveled tens of miles to find the perfect tree, stopping once to cut down a pine on the side of a remote country road in the dark, after my husband failed to locate the lot we were seeking. He didn't want to disappoint our children. Feeling guilty about the deed, Rick had insisted we go back in the spring, also after dark, and plant a sapling.

Buying a tree in a matter of minutes seems unnatural, but the frigid weather stifles any complaining. The kids are happy.

"Oh, Christmas tree. Oh, Christmas tree, I'm so glad Aunt Char found thee," Megan sings most of the way home, in between bouts of adoration for the evergreen.

"It's simply the most beautiful tree," she says.

As we near the house, Nick and Megan recount the story of our five mysterious gifts to their aunt and speculate on what the next present will be.

"Maybe there's a connection between the gifts in the song and the ones you're receiving," Char says. "What was gift number five—cards?"

"Angel note cards," Nick and Megan say together.

"In the song, the fifth gifts are golden rings," Char says. "Angels have halos? Those are like golden rings."

"That's right," Nick says. "But I don't see the connection between the partridge in a pear tree and a poinsettia."

"The tree and the plant both have green leaves," Megan says. "And they both begin with the letter *P*."

"What about the other gifts? Any more connections?" Char asks.

"We got two bags of bows on the second day," Megan says. "The bags had two bows of each color, including red, green, blue, and white, like turtle doves. But what do three rolls of gift wrap have to do with French hens?"

"Who knows?" Char says. "It's a puzzle, though, and you two are good at those."

We spot the package on the front porch just as Char turns the truck into the driveway. Nick is out of the vehicle before it rolls to a full stop.

"We got another one," he shouts.

The gift bag holds six plastic drinking cups and a homemade card.

"Everyone into the house," Nick says. "Let's look for clues."

I halt the procession.

"Let's unload the tree first."

"Where's your tree stand?" Char asks. "We can take this baby right inside and set it up."

"It's in the garage. I'll get it."

Megan is racing around the garage to the back door, when I remember that our Christmas tree stand is history, thanks to my demolition derby a few nights ago.

"Wait. Come back," I holler, and Megan returns. "Let's put the tree in the garage. Give it a day or two to thaw."

I leave the three of them waiting outside, while I go through the house to open the big garage door. I hide the smashed tree stand under some tarps, before flipping the switch to open the door.

"Took you long enough," Char says, under her breath. "Hiding presents in there?"

It takes all four of us to haul the stiff tree out of the back of the truck. Once in the garage, I hold the spindly evergreen up, while Nick and Megan try to loosen the branches. A limb snaps off in Nick's hand.

"Oops."

Char instructs us to lean the fuller side of the tree against the garage wall. That's when I realize how pathetic our little tree really is. The branches are bending at a near ninety-degree angle, and many of the tips hang by thin strings of bark. Even Megan wrinkles her nose a bit at our purchase.

"If the other side doesn't fluff out, at least they'll be even," she says, making us all laugh.

Exhausted from a day of Christmas shopping, Char leaves us to solve the mystery of the gifts on our own. Nick collects the cards and lays them out on the dining room table.

The newest addition, four-by-three inches on white construction paper, is the smallest we've received. The design, like the ones that came with earlier gifts, includes hand-drawn holly leaves.

"Whoever is making the cards is an artist," Megan says. "That's one thing I know for sure."

"Are either of you close to an art teacher?" I ask.

"Mrs. Urschel is a wonderful artist," Megan says. "Remember when I wanted to quit school in first grade to become an artist? She taught mc I could do both."

"Have you talked to her lately? Does she even know about your dad?"

"She's at the elementary school. I can't remember the last time I saw her."

"We're never going to figure this out," Nick says after a few more minutes. "I'm going downstairs to see what else needs to be done in the basement."

Megan and I follow him down.

"A second coat of paint," I say. "That ought to do it."

I leave the painting to Nick and Megan. Using Christmas shopping as an excuse to get out of the house, I have to buy a new tree stand. By the time I get to the hardware store, the manager is locking the doors, so I drive to the twenty-four-hour discount center.

"Sold our last stand this afternoon."

Running out of options, I call my brother-in-law Tom.

"I've got an old stand in the garage. It's rickety, but it'll work."

A light snow begins falling during the short drive to my in-laws. Tom meets me at the garage door with the rusted stand in hand.

"Rick bought a new one of these last year. I was with him," he says thoughtfully.

Mercifully, Tom doesn't ask what happened to the new stand.

Ten minutes later, I'm stopped at Little Sugarcreek and Feedwire Roads on my way home, when a red car streaks through the intersection. A hand sticks out of the open window on the passenger side holding a lighted cigarette. Even though my car windows are rolled up, I hear music blasting from the vehicle: Pantera's *The Great Southern Trendkill*. It's Ben's favorite album.

My eyes follow the car as it leaps into the air at the crest of the first in a series of mogul-like hills. Belly-drop hills, the police call them, because that's what happens if you drive over them too fast.

The car behind me honks, and I move on, but I don't go home. I turn right and follow in the direction of the car, fearing that Ben is the driver. Hoping I am wrong. My hands tremble on the steering wheel as my car creeps over the first hill, then the second. There is no wreckage on the roadside, no smoke rising from a bent engine. No bodies.

I tell myself Ben is safe at a friend's house. They are watching movies, playing video games, eating junk food. But I don't know for sure. I never catch up with the car. Its taillights are swallowed by darkness and snowfall.

When I finally turn my car around and head for home, I can't help but think of the gift givers, hoping their Christmas spirit will touch Ben's heart just as it has Nick's and Megan's.

Chapter Seven

The Seventh Day of Christmas

The clock on the mantel chimes twice: two a.m. I stand at the window watching the darkened street, praying every time I see headlights creeping toward the house that they will be Ben's. I have been worried ever since I saw the red car speeding through the intersection on the way home from Tom's house.

There have been too many nights like this, with me waiting at the window, enforcing no consequences when Ben comes home way later than his midnight curfew. I'm so afraid of driving him further away from me that I stay mute, not giving my son what I know he needs—parenting and love.

Shame on me.

Since Rick's death, I have been emotionally absent from our children, blind to Nick's nightmares, unable to fill Megan's need for Christmas. Ben is drifting, walking alone with his grief.

If someone had asked me how we were getting along a week

ago, I would have said fine, under the circumstances. I work. Pay bills. The kids attend school. Most days, someone remembers to feed the dog and cat.

But we weren't fine, and our true friends knew it.

Now I do, too.

I have been sleepwalking for more than two months, hardly conscious of a family falling apart. It wasn't until I nearly stumbled over that poinsettia that I began to see how much my kids needed me.

My eyes are open now.

Thanks to our true friends, Momma Bear is back. My gusto for Christmas may not be the same as in years past, but my kids will know they are not on their own. We'll order a pizza. I'll buy a few presents, and we will decorate our tree, provided it thaws out.

I flip the porch light on and off to make sure it is working, then patrol the house, careful not to wake Megan and Nick, who went to bed hours ago. When I reach my own closed bedroom door, I hesitate. I haven't been in there for weeks. My clothes hang on a rack in the laundry room. I sleep on the couch. I shower in the guest bathroom. Though I tell myself there is nothing to be afraid of, the room frightens me. I have not dusted in there or vacuumed since before October 8.

Placing my hand on the doorknob, I find myself wishing one of those true friends were here beside me now. The thought surprises me, and I don't feel so alone. I was angry when we received that first gift, now I am curious about who they are and grateful for their attention.

This room is another demon they will help me conquer.

The hinges of the door squeak as I push it open. I peek inside from the safety of the hallway, where the chill of the room is already starting to creep.

I force myself to see what my children see every time I send one of them in here to fetch a blouse from the closet, or a necklace from my jewelry box. I always have an excuse not to go myself; tonight, as I wait for my son to come home, there are no more excuses.

A thick layer of dust covers the pine frame of our king-sized waterbed. The fitted sheet Rick died on is still tucked around the mattress. His too-small slippers, with the smashed-down heels, sit next to the bathroom door. The gym bag my husband planned to pack for his hospital stay stands empty in the corner.

It is as if the room is waiting.

I tug the sheet off the bed, the pillowcases, the blankets, and stuff them into the gym bag. They will go, unwashed, to Goodwill. I fetch one of the boxes Megan emptied of Christmas decorations from the family room and carry it upstairs. The old slippers go in first, then I thin out Rick's closet of everything except his favorite sweaters. Those I leave hidden among my own clothes. Rick's watch, Swiss Army knife, key chain, and wedding ring go into the bottom of my jewelry box, keepsakes I will give to our kids someday. I find something else that needs to go; flushing the contents of four bottles of Rick's heart medication down the toilet seems an appropriate end. I toss the containers in the trash.

In less than half an hour, I have erased Rick's presence from the room. I have no idea what to do with the waterbed. I will never sleep on it again. I draw a heart in the dust with my finger on the top of its wooden frame and print Rick's initials inside it along with mine, then I wipe away the past with lemon furniture polish.

Tomorrow, I will ask Nick to help me drain the mattress. It's just a piece of plastic, but even it holds Christmas memories.

I can still see Ben, Nick, and Meg rushing in here on Christmas mornings to join their dad and me on this bed. After a late night of assembling trains or bikes or remote-control cars, Rick and I were usually still dozing when our Smith herd charged into the room. Pumping our water-filled mattress with their hands and knees, our kids would create a tsunami that forced us from slumber.

Small gifts stuffed into their Christmas stockings—candy, comic books, hair ribbons, maybe a wristwatch or baseball cards—got opened on our bed, while Rick waited for his coffee to brew and I for the tea kettle to boil.

Everyone would be wearing new pajamas, a tradition I started when the kids were small and began begging to open one gift on Christmas Eve. Rick always demanded the kids put on warm socks and brush their teeth, before visiting Santa land downstairs in the family room, building their anticipation.

When I hear the front door open, I go downstairs to talk with my Ben. I leave the bedroom door open, hoping life will spill back into the room.

Ben stands in the entryway, leaning his back against the door. A car drives by, and its headlights cast a ray of light around the room. I see tears glistening on my child's face. Mama Bear wants to step aside and let Mother Hen do thc talking, but I think we each could use a dose of both.

"I'm glad you're home."

Ben jumps, startled. He wipes at his face with the sleeve of his coat.

"What are you doing up?"

"Waiting for you."

"I'm tired. I need to go to bed."

Ben walks toward the steps. His intent, I'm sure, is to escape to the basement.

I block his path and give him a hug.

"Neither one of us can go on like this, Ben."

He tries to shake free, but I don't let him.

"Not tonight, Mom. Please, not tonight."

I pull back enough to look at his face, though he turns to avoid my gaze.

"I went to your uncle Tom's this evening. I was stopped at Little Sugarcreek when a red car flew through the intersection."

Ben doesn't admit he was the driver, but guilt flashes like a neon sign from the muscles in his jaw.

"Hand over your car keys."

"Mom . . ."

"Give them to me."

Ben holds the keys in his fist, debating, and then drops them into my open palm. He will never know my fear at that moment, while I waited to see whether he would comply or defy me. His acquiescence gives me grit to keep going.

"Now sit," I say. "You're going to tell me what you've been up to tonight."

We sit down on the couch. He says nothing.

"We can sit here all night," I say, nudging his shoulder with mine.

The words spill out, slow at first and then building speed as if he were still driving the car.

"I had to get out of here," he says. "I needed to drive. Robert came with me."

"Where'd you go?"

"You're not going to like it."

"You're probably right."

Ben tells me he kept a close eye on the speedometer as he cruised residential streets toward the hills on Little Sugarcreek Road. Out in the country, the hum of the car engine turned into a roar.

"I could drive that road with my eyes closed," he says. "I must have driven it one hundred times with Dad."

Ben tells me that he and Robert rolled down their windows and let blasts of wet December wind smack their faces.

"When the car jumped over the first hill, I felt like I was flying," he says. "We were screaming this song."

"Pantera. *Great Southern Trendkill*," I say.

"Yeah, from that album. How'd you know?"

"I heard it."

Ben makes a face, but he continues with the confession.

A mile or two passes before he turns onto an open stretch of country road: no hills, no stop signs, and not much traffic. If homeowners glanced out their windows as the car passed, all they would have seen is the red glow of his taillights.

"When the speedometer hit ninety, I wasn't afraid or sad. I felt free."

I clasp my hands together, willing them to stop shaking, and then ask, "What made you slow down?"

"You won't believe it."

"Try me."

"It was Dad."

Ben tells me that he and Robert, in unison, spotted a deer leap across a fence and stop in the road just ahead of them.

"I could hear Dad's voice telling me to downshift and hit the brakes. Then as fast as that deer appeared . . . it was gone. There was no crash, just twenty feet of tire burn. Dad was there in the car with me, Mom, just like before."

I wrap an arm around Ben and pull him close. This time, I know what to say.

"Your Dad is always going to be with us. He's probably listening right now and wondering if I'm ever going to give you back these car keys."

We sit quietly for a few minutes, but Ben wants an answer.

"So, are you?"

I toss the keys up in the air just out of his reach, and I catch them.

"Red Baron's grounded until the first of the year, then we're going to have a talk with the guidance counselor at the high school. "

Ben starts to argue, but changes his mind.

We talk a while longer, but our conversation turns into a duel of yawns.

"Bed?" I ask.

While I lock the front door, Ben notices the empty tree stand in the corner.

"So the tree shopping was a bust?"

"Not with your aunt Char in change. It's in the garage thawing."

"Out there with our busted tree stand?"

No use lying. I am caught.

"You saw that?"

"One of the legs wasn't completely smashed. Ran over it a couple of times myself."

For the first time, maybe ever, my teenage son and I understand each other.

We head off to bed laughing.

I wake to the aromas of a picnic in the woods: fresh pine and frying bacon. It's only been a few hours since Ben and I retired for the night, but a whispered conversation up in the kitchen clues me in to the fact that my eldest son and his little sister are awake. The two of them are cooking up something that Ben doesn't want me to know about.

"Keep it down. You'll wake her," he says with a voice so deep it bellows down the stairwell. Megan giggles.

"I can't wait for her to see it. I just can't wait," she says.

Figuring I'm about to be served breakfast in bed—or, on couch, such as it is—I close my eyes and relax, until they decide it's time to eat. I figure Ben is trying to earn back his car keys. I won't tell him it's not going to work until after the meal. I close my eyes and drift back to sleep.

A half hour later, Megan holds a slice of cooked bacon under my nose.

When I open my eyes, she eats the meat and then runs back upstairs hollering, "Breakfast."

Upstairs, it's not the eggs, or the bacon, or even the toast that surprises me. It's the tree. Our somewhat lopsided evergreen stands in front of the living room window, covered in strands of tiny white lights.

"Who did this?"

Megan beams. "It was Ben."

Beside the tree, a box labeled "Dad's stuff" stands empty, except for Rick's measuring tape.

Rick had been the tree-lighting aficionado of the family, with arms long enough to reach to the very top of any tree, a feat he ensured before the purchase of a pine. He painstakingly untangled the mess of twisted strands that I had hastily packed the previous year. Once assured every bulb lighted, Rick measured the distance between light strings as he wrapped them around the tree. He would have measured the distance between ornaments if I had let him.

Less than twenty-four hours ago, Ben was disavowing all things holiday related. Today he's lighting the tree. I should be shocked, but I'm not. Unexpected events are becoming the norm in our house, especially when it comes to Christmas.

"You did this?" I ask Ben. I want to hear it from him.

Ben leaves the room for a moment and comes back holding one of the six cups from the gift givers, filled with orange juice.

"They've been trying to help us through Christmas. My attitude has been . . . sort of . . . undermining their efforts," he says. "Next year, we can all put the lights on the tree together. This time, I needed it to be just me and Dad."

I nod an affirmative to Ben and take deep breaths so I don't cry.

"Don't you go getting another cold," Megan says. "It's way too close to Christmas."

"Do you like the tree by the picture window, instead of downstairs in the family room like always?" Ben asks. "I think it makes the house merrier from the outside."

"When did my kids get so smart?" I ask myself, then to Ben, "Good job."

"How about we eat," he says, and then he shouts a warning to his sleeping brother. "Bacon will be gone in sixty seconds."

Nick is the first one seated at the table.

Use of the plastic Christmas cups with our morning meal turns all our thoughts to the identity of our true friends and the gift we expect to receive sometime today.

"What's the seventh gift in the song?" Megan asks, but none of us is sure.

Nick volunteers to look up the lyrics to "The Twelve Days of Christmas" after the last piece of bacon disappears off the plate. He prints out a copy of the song and returns to the table, where Ben, Megan, and I are still debating whether one of their art teachers could be a suspect. Refusing to sing the words of the song as his sister requests, Nick reads off the list of gifts.

"Seven swans a-swimming, eight maids a-milking, nine ladies dancing, ten lords a-leaping, eleven pipers piping, and twelve drummers drumming. Geez, definitely not what I would be sending to a true love."

We all stare at Nick. My mouth is hanging open.

"So, what would you be sending, and to whom?" Ben asks, but we all want to know.

"Not saying I plan to send anything to anybody, but if I did, I'd send cool stuff: candy, video games, DVDs."

"That would be awfully expensive," I say. "I like the gifts

we've been receiving. They're big enough to show someone cares without being too much."

Nick mulls over the idea.

"Just in case we get Swedish fish or Goldfish crackers tonight, instead of seven swimming swans, I got dibs," he says.

I volunteer to wash the dishes and send the kids to their rooms with plastic bags to fill with any outgrown clothes or toys. I plan to make a trip to the Goodwill donation trailer today to deposit the items we boxed up from the basement and Rick's things. I don't want to give myself a chance to change my mind and keep them.

I'm clearing away the remains of our breakfast, when I get a telephone call from an old friend of Rick's. Terry Molnar had worked at Gem City Engineering with my husband for years.

"The guys at the shop bought some Christmas presents for the kids. I'd like to drop them off."

We arrange to meet later in the week. I don't mention the anonymous gifts or the cards. I decide to wait until Terry's here at the house to tell him about them, so I can see his reaction.

It's all beginning to make sense.

I can't believe I never considered the guys from Gem City as our gift givers. Rick had worked there for more than twenty years. Many of his coworkers had also been close friends.

I decide to keep my suspicions to myself. If I'm right, I don't want to spoil the surprise for the kids. Before Terry's arrival, I will grant one of Megan's Christmas wishes. I will bring our collection of Santa figures out of hiding tomorrow.

❄

It's nearly four o'clock by the time I load the trunk of my car with our giveaways and drive to Goodwill. The donation trailer is locked, but people have stacked an assortment of bags and boxes filled with clothes, toys, and household bric-a-brac underneath the trailer to give them protection from the weather.

A man is digging through the stockpile.

Holding a doll with wild white hair, he spits on his finger and tries to wipe a smudge off its face. I assume it didn't work. He tosses the doll back into a box and continues his search.

I'm unsure whether to get out of the car or wait until he leaves. Then I get an idea. I walk over and talk to him.

"How old is your daughter?" I ask.

He stands up and turns to face me.

"She's eight," he says, looking down. "Did something stupid at work. Lost my job. I was hoping to find something to put under the tree."

"Any luck?"

He shakes his head.

"Most of what people give, no one would want."

I had felt that way a few days ago, and suddenly I am overwhelmed by a desire to make sure this man knows he is not the only one feeling desperate during these holidays.

I tell him about the gifts we've been receiving, the cards, the mystery, my anger when we found the poinsettia, and how I packed up the sheets my husband died on last night. He listens even though an icy wind blows and large, wet snowflakes are falling. I speak with no pauses, just words strung together like rosary beads.

When I finally take a breath, he looks at me and smiles.

"I guess some gifts are worth giving," he says.

He extends a hand for me to shake. "My name is Charles."

"I'm Jo. How about you help me unload some things from my trunk?"

Charles follows me over to the car. We unload bags from the basement first, then my bedroom. I save a Hello Kitty beach bag stuffed with a cornucopia of Megan's outgrown girly apparel: fuzzy pink pajamas, skirts, a few sweaters, blue jeans, and basketball shorts. A bracelet-making kit that my daughter never opened, several stuffed animals, and a book on hair braiding stick out of the top.

The man looks at me and says, "Wow."

"I've done some stupid things in my life, too," I tell him.

"You don't mind if I take these home?"

"I would mind if you didn't."

He stands rummaging through the bag, then stops and says, "Merry Christmas."

For the first time this holiday season, I say the same.

"Merry Christmas, Charles. "

The words feel right.

When I return home, the house is empty. I go down to the basement, look in the bedrooms. Not a creature is stirring.

I check the garage. The engine on Ben's car is cold, so I go back into the house and punch his cell number into my phone. I hear it ringing faintly, then the clatter of footsteps on the roof.

Raccoons had raided bags of stale bread from a neighbor's

garbage last summer, choosing our roof as their banquet hall and their commode. It was disgusting. Rick and I had walked the block asking neighbors to place heavy rocks on their trash cans to prevent the little rascals from getting inside. With their food supply cut off, the raccoons got the message and moved on.

My first thought when I hear the noise on the roof: they're back.

I run to the back door via the dining room but find a ladder is blocking my exit. I can't open the door without knocking it down, and I panic thinking my children may be on the roof trying to shoo away an animal that could carry rabies.

Outside, I find reindeer and raccoons aren't the only animals taken with rooftops.

Nick is climbing over the roof near the ridge. Ben stands at the top of the extension ladder, evidently giving his brother directions. My sweet little Megan is holding the ladder steady.

Nick has been a roof climber since before he turned five. He never needed a ladder; he had death-gripping toes and strong arms. It had scared me breathless the first time I caught him up there, but I've gotten used to it over the years; when he was little he called the roof his "office." He's always climbing something, but I draw the line at the rooftop in winter.

"Everybody freeze."

Nick loses his footing and slides. My heart jumps out of my chest, but he just laughs.

"Whoaaaa," he says, stopping his fall just above the gutters. He chooses to shimmy down a deck post instead of using the ladder, which is still occupied by Ben.

"I told you it wouldn't be bad," Ben says, addressing his

brother as if I wasn't there. "It's not that slippery, and it's snowing."

Megan looks at me and wilts.

"I told them not to do it. I told them you would be angry."

"Don't be such a baby," Ben says. "How was it, Nick?"

"Perfect. Had a great view in both directions. I'd have seen Mom pull up, if I had gotten to the ridge before she got home."

I can't believe what I'm hearing. They continue chatting about the vantage point from the roof as if it's perfectly natural.

"Time out," I shout.

The kids stop strategizing and look at me.

"You," I say pointing at Ben and Nick, "put the ladder back in the garage, then all of you into the house, *now*."

By the time the trio is seated on the couch, my heart is back where it belongs, but I'm angry at their recklessness.

"What were you thinking?"

They confess together.

Ben had summoned Nick and Megan down to his room for a strategy session to figure out how to catch our true friends in the act.

"We need a way to watch for them, without them knowing," Nick had said. "We don't want them to stop leaving the gifts."

Ben comes up with two ideas: lie low on the floor of the garage with the big door open just enough to watch for cars, or go up on the roof.

Nick volunteers to take the high road.

"I told him it could be slippery," Ben says, as if to make me feel better. "We were testing it out."

Rick and I had taught our kids to be adventurous—hiking in

the mountains, camping in the wilderness—and I feel somewhat responsible for their actions today. I have a feeling Rick would have been up there on the roof with them, if he had been here.

It's Megan who realizes I'm not paying attention to the conversation.

"Earth to Mom?"

"We need to figure out when to go up. I don't want to be lying on the roof any longer than I have to," Nick says.

He still thinks this is going to happen. My children are crazy if they think I'm going to let them go up on a snowy roof at night, but maybe a stakeout by the garage door isn't such a bad idea. I want to know who is leaving the gifts just as much as they do. I could layer the concrete floor with sleeping bags and blankets, make hot chocolate. It could be fun and we'd be together.

"Hellooo, don't you think the gift givers will notice someone lying on the roof?" I ask.

"They'll probably just think I'm a Christmas decoration," Nick says.

"If you want to catch our friends, figure out a safe way to do it. Maybe tomorrow we can try Ben's alternate plan."

The boys head to the basement, and I fear another conspiracy may be afoot. Megan hangs out with me.

"Maybe we'll have a snow day tomorrow," she says hopefully. "Snow days all the way to Christmas break would be lovely."

"Is it still snowing?" I ask.

Megan opens the front door and flips on the porch light. A small package sits in the snow outside the door.

"It's here! The seventh gift!"

Ben and Nick hear Megan's announcement and race back

upstairs to confiscate the card. A debonair little snowman with a colorful string scarf and big red shoes smiles at us from the front cover. Inside, there are pictures of pine trees, and our family's special version of the Christmas carol.

On the Seventh Day
of Christmas
Your true friends give to you . . .
Seven golden apples
Six holiday cups
Five angeled note cards
Four gift boxes
Three rolls of gift wrap
Two bags of bows
and
One poinsettia
For all of you

I let the boys fuss over the card. I'm pretty sure Terry's visit later in the week will end the mystery, at least for me.

My daughter is admiring the seven gold apple ornaments, when Nick tries to grab them from her.

"Let's put them on the tree," he says.

She refuses to give them up.

"These are special," she says. "I know where they belong, and it's not on the tree."

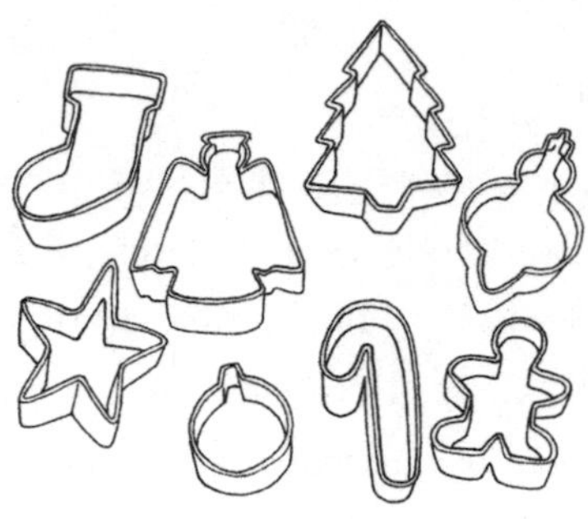

Chapter Eight
The Eighth Day of Christmas

With Megan overseeing our progress, the transformation of our home from everyday to holiday is nearly complete. It has taken an all-out Smith family effort to accomplish. By late afternoon the day after the golden apples arrive, I am surveying the house room by room, making sure it's ready for our first holiday guest. Rick's friend and coworker Terry Molnar is on his way.

Megan and I have exhumed my collection of Santa figurines, who now stand at attention on the sideboard in the living room. The ones that don't fit are spreading the spirit of the season in some unexpected spaces. Made of glass, carved from chestnut, molded in porcelain and plastic, or hand sewn, each figure is a vessel of Christmas memories. A foot-tall Santa dressed in a green coat flashes the peace sign from behind a shower curtain in the guest bathroom, and I park a rotund Père Noël beside our bathroom scale, a reminder not to overindulge.

❄

Rick and I had few contentious moments in our marriage, but the extent of my Santa collection definitely created several.

Once, as we were packing the figurines away for the season, Rick asked me which of the jolly old elves was my favorite. We were running out of storage space in the basement, and he thought it time to thin down the collection. I looked around: my sister Carol—Aunt Sugar to my kids because she always carried candy for them in her purse—had made weekly payments on the hand-carved, pipe-toting Santa dressed in red long johns. She believed paying for presents on the installment plan kept loved ones close to her heart all through the year, or at least until their gifts were paid off.

Her motto: "I don't just give gifts, I make memories."

Not all of my Santas are store-bought; several of my favorites are made of construction paper and cotton balls, presents from my children in the early stages of their artistic careers. Rick gave me only one, a weary little fellow with sad eyes. The blue-robed Saint Nick always seemed out of step with the rest of the happy crowd, and I asked my husband why he had selected that particular one for me.

"He carries the burdens of the world, so the rest of us don't have to," Rick had said. "Give him troubles. Give me your troubles."

Then he had kissed me and whispered, "I love you."

❄

As the origin of each Santa pinballed around in my brain, I realized Rick's question wasn't that difficult to answer.

"All of them," I said.

Rick had thrown up his hands then at the thought of finding room to store my seven boxes of chubby little dudes. He was the closet organizer, the cupboard cleaner, the guy who drew a diagram to pack a suitcase or rearrange furniture. I'm more of a "shove, stuff, and close the door quickly" kind of girl.

"You want me reorganizing the storage closet?" I had asked.

"My place in the family, right?" he had said.

I gave him a polite "yes dear," and handed him the largest box.

This year I will repack the decorations myself, but I have the feeling his spirit will be standing there with me, especially if I fall back on my stuff-and-slam method. And while it's painful to think about, I realize that I will cherish the moments that remind me of him.

I rearrange several of the Santas, then do a 360-degree scan around the room. The evergreen illuminating the front window still needs trimming, but the lights make the room festive. Nick has fashioned the pine sprigs that broke off its frozen trunk into a centerpiece for the table. I dig out a peppermint-scented candle and place it amid the greenery. When I light it, the minty aroma fills the house.

"Smells like candy canes," Megan says, surveying the room approvingly. "We should buy some."

I had driven to Bellbrook Chocolates earlier in the day and had walked right past a display of candy canes on my way to purchase six boxes of candy for Terry to bring back to the folks at Gem City. I don't want to seem ungrateful if they are the source of our mysterious gifts.

"Next time I go to the grocery," I promise my daughter.

Megan insists on greeting our guest in a too-small red sweater adorned with a polar bear dressed in Santa attire. The sleeves miss her wrists by two inches. I try to coax her into a lovely purple sweatshirt I bought last fall.

"This is the only Christmas sweater I have," she says, folding her arms across her chest. "I'm wearing it."

The boys are less concerned about their appearance. They wear dress shirts scented with Easy-On Speed Starch. I add extra under-eye concealer to my makeup regime.

Earlier in the day, I had scrubbed the family room floor, the kitchen, the bathrooms. I want Terry to see a mother in charge, a family recovering, kids under control. We are not perfect, but we are better. Christmas is hard work; I'm tired but also energized. If we learn Rick's coworkers are orchestrating this game of Secret Santa for our family, I want them to know they have made a difference. I half expect the lot of them to show up on our doorstep, just like the gifts.

Even Ben agrees to be part of the welcoming committee, and I wonder if he shares my suspicions that his father's coworkers are not just being friendly, but are true friends.

"I want to hear what Terry has to say" is all he acknowledges.

In the kitchen, my eldest and I fill green and red bowls with chips and pretzels for our guest. The offerings look paltry on the dining room table.

"We should have baked cookies," Ben says.

I look at him and raise my eyebrow to say that none of us could have fit another chore into this day.

"Next year," I tell him. "We'll make cookies."

He is fiddling with a twisty tie on the potato chip bag, but the darn thing keeps falling off. When it lands on the floor a third time, I pick it up.

"What's on your mind, Kiddo?"

I rethink the old nickname when Ben lifts his face and looks at me. The maturity I see chiseled there is a new work of art.

"It won't be long before he leaves me, too," I say to myself. "But he will come back . . . with a wife, maybe grandchildren."

"Is Christmas always going to be this hard?" he asks quietly. "We won't have the gift givers to help us through the holidays next year. How do we make it without them, without Dad?"

"We're learning," I tell him.

We lean into each other.

"We will hold each other up."

The doorbell rings, and we step away from each other.

"Let's go meet our gift givers," I say.

"You really think it's the guys from Gem City?"

"Yep. We'll know for sure in a minute."

But Terry arrives alone, carrying Christmas stockings filled with candy, small toys, and gadgets for the kids. Though he has been my friend for more than twenty years, Rick was our connection. My husband's absence makes the conversation between us awkward.

"I remember when I first met him," Terry says, still standing by the door. "I went over to his house on a Friday night with his brother Tom. Rick was sitting cross-legged on the floor in between two huge stereo speakers. He was bouncing up and down to the beat of the music. I've never laughed so hard. I just loved him."

Megan sits on the couch beaming, her large smile encouraging Terry to share more tales of her dad.

"Please, let me take your coat. Sit down," I say.

Terry shakes his head.

"I can't stay long."

He pulls an envelope from his coat pocket and hands it to me.

"This is from the guys at the shop."

The envelope bulges with cash and gift certificates to a local superstore, one that carries everything from groceries to electronics and toys. Terry tells us the company gave the gift certificates to its employees as a Christmas bonus. Eighty-eight people had regifted them to us.

The idea started with Steve Hey, a Gem City employee who had worked for Rick for many years. In the weeks following his boss's death, I learned Steve had replayed old messages left by Rick on his answering machine just to hear his voice.

When Steve shared the idea of taking up a collection for us, the shipping department built ten wooden donation boxes and painted them red. The design team created signs for the boxes, which were placed throughout the shop.

During this season when most people were counting their pennies to fulfill the holiday dreams of their own children, the people at Gem City had remembered mine.

"This means so much," I say. "Thank you."

"Buy something special for the kids this Christmas," Terry says.

Nick doesn't hide his enthusiasm.

"That's a great idea."

Terry laughs. "He's just like his dad."

My mind is blank as new paper. I forget the refreshments out in the kitchen. Thankfully, Ben is thinking more clearly.

"We didn't have time to bake cookies, but we have some chips."

"I'm good. Thanks."

I set the envelope down on the coffee table and walk Terry outside. As I exit the room, I imagine Nick mentally calculating the contents of the envelope based on size and approximate weight. I know Ben is holding him back.

We hear a scuffle as we walk out the door, and I suspect the kids are diving for the envelope. Terry and I both smile. He hugs me good-bye.

"I was on sick leave the day Rick died. They called me at home," he says. "When I heard, I just sat there in the chair. I can't even tell you what I thought."

Terry leaves me standing on the front porch. As he opens his car door, I remember there's a question I haven't asked him. I think about calling out to him, but change my mind.

"If the gifts stop now, I will know," I whisper, and somehow talking to myself doesn't seem so worrisome anymore.

By the time I step back inside, Ben and Nick are separating the cash into similar denominations. All total, Rick's Gem City family gave us $3,453 in cash and certificates.

"This is freakin' awesome," Ben says. "I can't believe it."

Megan kneels on the couch watching as her daddy's buddy drives off.

"They really liked him, didn't they?" she asks.

I sit beside her, picking cat hair from her sweater.

"He was easy to love."

Ben stops counting the cash after a third tally and asks if I mentioned the anonymous gifts. I'm embarrassed to say no.

"Do you suppose this is it? Are the gifts history?" he asks.

"It's only the eighth day of Christmas. Our true friends would never stop now," Megan says confidently.

While the boys begin debating how the money should be spent, I stuff it all back into the envelope.

"We should do something special for the people who gave it to us," Megan says, and I agree.

"Send a thank-you note," Nick suggests. "Thank goodness you're a writer, Mom."

"My place in the family, right?" I say, echoing Rick's words.

How do you thank someone for supporting your children through the worst Christmas of their lives? Eight days ago the world looked different. I thought we were alone. Today, I know true friends surround us. The kindness shown to our family humbles me. I drop spare change in the Salvation Army kettle every Christmas, but I've never really gone out of my way to help anyone. I'm not a bad person; I just never thought about what it means to be good. Is it really giving if it comes easy? I don't think so anymore.

Nick pulls me back into the conversation.

"Are you going to do it, Mom? Are you going to let us pick something special out for Christmas, like Terry said?"

"Maybe, but there's something I want each of you to do first."

A trio of groans interrupts me.

"No more housework," Nick pleads. "The floors squeak they're so clean."

I have something else in mind.

"People have been so generous to us since Daddy died, cooking meals, shuttling you guys to practices. Now we have this wonderful gift from Gem City and the others from our true friends. How about we try to do something that honors them all? Let's make Christmas merry for someone else."

I watch as the three kids mull it over. Ben speaks up first.

"I'm going to need cash," he says reaching for the envelope from Gem City in my hand. "It takes money to make merry."

That's not what I'm going for here.

"It doesn't have to involve money, or presents. When you see someone in need, don't walk away. Do something."

Megan likes the idea.

Nick rejects it outright.

"I don't know anybody who needs anything."

My stomach growls, reminding me that I haven't eaten since breakfast, but I don't want to let this conversation drop.

"How about we go out to dinner and talk about it?"

"That'll give our gift givers the opportunity to drop off today's present," Megan says. "Let's get Italian. That's Dad's favorite."

The idea is tempting, but I take a different approach. I grab paper and pencils from the junk drawer and give one of each to the kids.

"Everybody write down your favorite restaurant."

We put our selections into Ben's baseball cap, and then I reach in and pick one.

"Ponderosa."

All three cheer. I take a peek at the other selections for future reference. They are all the same. Ben grabs the car keys from my purse, tosses them in the air, and catches them.

"Can I drive?"

We wait in line at the restaurant for half an hour, then grab a table so far away from the buffet line that Nick insists he will need to consume extra carbs to compensate for the walk. We lay our coats over the chairs so other table hunters will know this one is occupied. Nick, naturally, is the first in line and the first to return to our table. I take my time making food selections, lots of salad, a baked potato, and my absolute favorite, brussels sprouts. I am so focused on the feast before me, I don't immediately notice the young man wearing military fatigues sitting at our table until he stands and pulls out the chair for me.

"How do, ma'am," he says.

It's been a long time since I've been the recipient of such chivalry. It is nice, but I'm not sure why this soldier is seated at our table.

Nick swallows a mouthful of mashed potatoes and then introduces me to his new friend John.

"He was standing in the corner, and his plate of food was getting cold. He had no place to sit," Nick says. "We had an empty chair."

Nick goes back into food-shoveling mode, this time attacking a plate of chicken wings.

"I don't want to be a bother," John says apologetically. "It's just that Nick here, he insisted."

"Please, join us!" I motion for him to sit down, smiling to myself that despite his earlier protest, Nick obviously did know how to reach out to others. "Sit. Eat."

As we eat, John tells us his family lives nearby. Granted leave two days ago, he had planned to surprise his mother.

"I took a cab from the airport. No one was home," he says. "Food sounded like a good way to pass time, so I walked over."

John's excitement over seeing his family grows more evident as we get to know him.

"Mom was disappointed when I told her I might not make it home for the holidays," he says. "The whole family goes caroling on Christmas Eve, except for her. She stays home, roasting the turkey, making homemade dressing, all the trimmings."

He grows quiet, but his smile broadens. When he speaks again, his eyes are closed.

"The smell of our house on Christmas Eve sticks in my memory more than any present I ever received. That's home to me. That's the holidays."

The kids remain quiet while John sits with eyes closed. Even Nick sets his fork down and stops munching.

John's memories draw me back to my own childhood and the meals my mom prepared on Christmas Eve. Fried white-fish, Polish sausage, cabbage rolls. The feast was a precursor to midnight mass, where Mom sang Polish Christmas carols with the choir. Though my dad, who was of Hungarian descent, didn't understand a word of the lyrics, he had memorized them over the years and belted them out as if native-born.

I am wondering what holiday memory will linger with my kids, when John opens his eyes and catches us staring at him.

"Sorry," he says. "Who wants dessert?"

The kids flock to the buffet line. That's when John asks me about their dad.

"Was he sick long?"

I don't want to go there. I don't want to be sad or feel bad about how much I am enjoying this evening. But Rick is part of our story, and I can't deny his existence any more than John could forget his mom.

"He was sicker than I realized," I finally say. "This is our first Christmas without him."

John places his hand over mine and says, "That's tough, but I can see you're strong. My dad died the year I graduated high school. I wanted to kick the whole world that first Christmas. Mom wouldn't let me. She told me to remember the good times."

Ben, Nick, and Megan file back into their seats with bowls of chocolate pudding, ice cream smothered in hot fudge, and a variety of cobblers, which Megan declares is a healthy dish because it contains fruit. I have my doubts.

"Somebody's going to be sick."

"Not a chance," Nick says. "I could eat a ton of this stuff."

Megan eats about half of her cobbler, then pushes it away and looks at us expectantly.

"We should get going. We might have a gift waiting at home for us."

We tell John about the anonymous gifts and our hope to pass on Christmas cheer to others this year.

"That's why I invited you to join us," Nick says. "You were alone. We weren't."

"Thank you," John says. "It's been fun, a night to remember."

Nick holds his stomach and grimaces. "I'd like to forget some of those chicken wings."

Our dinner ends quickly with my son's next announcement.

"I'm going to explode," he declares. "Better get me home."

We offer John a ride.

"I've got to walk off these wings," he says. "It's just a few blocks."

"What if your mom's not home?" Ben asks.

"I have a key. If she doesn't show up soon, I'll call her."

We turn toward the car, but John holds me back.

"Remember the good times," he says. "Merry Christmas."

❄

We're nearly home when I notice a car pulling away from the curb just past our driveway.

"Follow it," Nick shouts from the backseat. "It's gotta be them."

Ben speeds up, but I caution him not to get too close.

"We don't want to give ourselves away."

Nick and Megan order me to slump down in the front seat, so I won't be recognized. They do the same in the back. Nick tosses a crumb-coated knit cap from his coat pocket to Ben to wear as camouflage.

"Dude, where has this thing been?" Ben asks, refusing to wear it. "It smells like cereal."

Nick grabs a handful of the crud from his pocket and sniffs it, then tastes a sliver.

"Cinnamon Toast Crunch," he says.

Ben reminds Nick that he's supposed to be sick.

"Take a right. Take a right," Nick hollers inches from Ben's ears. "They're turning."

"Looks like a Chevy, older model," I say, but Ben thinks it's a Ford. Neither of us is sure.

"It's blue," Megan whispers through the gap between my seat and the headrest. "Or maybe black or dark purple."

"Or maybe it's just dark outside," Ben says. "Put your seat belt back on."

"Go left. Go left." Nick again shouts driving directions, but he's been slumped behind the driver's seat and has missed the Volkswagen that turned in front of us, blocking our prey. He's watching the wrong vehicle.

We follow the car through Bellbrook neighborhoods, down Kensington Drive on to Clarkston, then Possum Run. We lose it, or maybe it loses us, at the stop sign on Little Sugarcreek Road. We drive around for half an hour but never spot the car again.

Finally, Megan calls off the search.

"Can't we just go home and see what they left us?"

"I should have kept my foot on the gas. We could have had them," Ben says.

I laugh off his comment.

"You're lucky to be driving at all."

Ben latches the safety locks on the car doors before we pull into the driveway, to prevent his brother and sister from bailing out before him. Once he releases the locks, all three run for the porch and the gift bag waiting there.

Megan reaches it first.

"Cookie cutters! Eight of them."

"*Really*," Ben says. "I mention our lack of cookies to Dad's friend, and we end up with a set of Christmas cookie cutters. That's no coincidence."

The card is different from the others; there are no fancy letters, no holly leaves or red-booted snowmen, just the words of the carol written in a neat cursive hand.

"It looks like one of your shopping lists," Megan says to me, then points out two misspelled words in the missive.

On the eigth day of Christmas . . .
your true friends give to you,
8 cookie cutters
7 golden apples
6 holiday cups
5 angel note cards
4 gift boxes
3 rolls of gift wrap
2 bags of bows
and . . .
1 Pointsettia
for all of you.

"I'll bet Terry rewrote the card after he left here," Ben says. "He probably had another gift in mind for today but bought the cookie cutters instead after he dropped off the envelope."

"That would explain why the card is so plain, no art," Nick agrees. "Didn't have time or art supplies to fancy it up."

We look for patterns in the cards and check for similar handwriting styles.

"It's funny when you think about it," Megan says. "We've been trying to figure out this mystery for eight days, and we never even asked Terry about the gifts. I think it's a sign."

"Okay, I'll bite," Ben says. "A sign of what?"

"That we're not supposed to know who they are."

"Hogwash."

All three kids look at me.

"Hog what?" Megan wants to know.

"If it takes me 'til Christmas, I'll find out who they are."

❄

It takes me less than two minutes to stash all of the homemade cards in my desk, so they don't disappear overnight, and add our new cookie cutters shaped like Santa boots, angels, evergreens, and ornaments to my already extensive collection in the kitchen. When I return to the living room, it's empty.

I hear the bass of Ben's stereo vibrating the walls of the basement stairwell and Super Mario music rings out from under the bathroom door. What I think is a Muppet singing a Christmas song wafts up from the television in the family room.

My children have gone their separate ways for the evening. Their disappearance is a letdown after the day we've spent together. I'm sitting on the couch alone when I get the idea.

Five minutes later, all the lights in the house go out at the same time.

"Looks like a power outage," I tell the kids when they join me in the living room. "Christmas lights must be putting a strain on the electric company."

"Do we have batteries so I can play my Game Boy?"

"Haven't bought any recently."

"Anybody seen my cell phone?" Ben feels around the dining room table where he remembers last seeing it, but it's not there.

We light lots of candles, but even reading is difficult in the dim light.

"How about we tell Christmas stories?" I suggest.

Ben groans. Megan is thrilled. Nick wants to go buy batteries.

"Did I ever tell you about the Christmas Dad bought me a typewriter?"

More groans. I ignore them.

"I had dreamed of becoming a writer since I was a little girl, and the gift was a show of support from your dad. He also told me that he feared success would change us, change me."

"He gave it to you anyway. That's a big deal," Ben says.

"It was a very big deal, but not in the way you might think. The *P* key on the machine was broken off. He told me, 'It's kind of a handicap, but I have confidence in you.'

"I was annoyed, but I took it as a challenge. And it was fun, you know, almost like a game that we played together while I was writing. A few months later, I found that broken *P* key in the lock box under the bed."

"I bet you were angry," Nick says. "What did you do?"

"I bought him a set of left-handed golf clubs at a garage sale the following year."

Their dad was right-handed, and he had laughed heartily when he opened the clubs and realized what I'd done. In the golf bag's special compartment for balls, he found my missing *P* key and a gift certificate for a set of right-handed clubs.

"I don't remember Dad buying a lot of Christmas presents, but the ones he gave were special, like my electric train set," Nick remembers. "He 'tested it out' for two days before he let me handle the controls."

He had tried doing the same when Ben got his first ten-speed bike, but his eldest hadn't fallen for it.

"He looked silly riding that bike. His knees hit the handlebars," Ben says. "He crashed it into a trash can on New Year's Day."

"Remember the butterfly clips he gave me last Christmas?" Megan asks. "He let me try them out in his hair."

Rick had come to Christmas breakfast wearing his new bathrobe with a dozen tiny braids in his short black hair. Megan had fastened a colorful clip to the end of each one.

"Not many dads would do that," she says.

We keep talking—about Rick, about Christmases and presents from the past. It is cozy, and even with the lights out I can feel a sense of being both merry and bright creeping into the house. Then Ben's cell phone rings.

"Jig's up," he says, when he sees it light up in my pocket.

"I'll go check the breaker box," I say, handing him the phone with a sigh. "I have a feeling the power is back on."

Chapter Nine

The Ninth Day of Christmas

My boss has been generous giving me time off work, so I don't argue when he turns down my request to stay home today. He wants me in the office writing "evergreens," or stories that can run anytime during the holidays.

"Everyone wants to be off this time of year," he says apologetically. "Newspapers don't close down for Christmas."

I'm reluctant to leave the kids, who are now on winter break, but I have little vacation time left this year. I decide to make the best of it and go in early. I stack several boxes of candy by the front door. They'll be gifts for my coworkers.

Ben is still sleeping, but I check in with my two younger children before leaving to hear their plans for the day.

"Not to worry," Nick says. "I've got my Game Boy and a box of cereal. I'm not getting outta bed."

"How about you help Megan decorate the tree."

"I'll supervise . . . from the couch . . . maybe."

I hear gift-wrapping sounds coming from Megan's bedroom, so I tap on her closed door and ask if she's hungry.

"Silly question, Momma," she says, jumping up from the floor and following me to the kitchen. "I'm always hungry."

With an elbow resting on the table and her head lounging in the palm of one hand, Megan shovels in mouthfuls of oatmeal with her free hand while sizing up the tree.

"It has potential. Just needs trimming."

Megan's favorite Christmas task has always been digging through our holiday tins to unearth the glass balls and bells and angels to hang on the tree. We like to joke that there's always an overabundance of ornaments on our tree right at her arm's length. In her excitement to unwrap these family treasures, she carpets the floor with the old newspapers and plastic grocery bags that I use to pack them away. She also usually manages to unravel rolls of ribbon or gift wrap in her enthusiasm to fashion homemade ornaments, and glitter becomes part of the upholstery.

The cleanup takes longer than the trimming.

Carrying one of the trinkets at a time was never sufficient for our daughter, even though the tins were only a few feet away. She insisted on an armful, and her breakage ratio was high. Inevitably, a snow globe or snowman would slip from her fingers, and her heart would ache for the loss of such beauty. Megan's many mishaps had led me to divide up our ornaments into precious and expendable years earlier. The really special ones she's not allowed to hang until she is older.

When she'd been much younger, Megan had convinced Rick to dig a grave in the backyard to bury a fallen angel ornament. She could not bear to see the delicate creature spending eternity in the trash.

From the kitchen window I had watched them standing together, saying a prayer over the tiny mound of earth next to the gym set. I was both envious of the moment they were sharing and filled with gratitude for my good luck.

He would have done anything for her, for all of us.

The incident touched him, too. He came back into the house changed.

Rick made it his parental mission to devise ways for our daughter to carry more than one ornament at a time. It was like the egg-drop experiment Ben did for science class, where students are asked to devise packaging to protect an egg from a one-story drop. Before tree-trimming night, I would buy a box of very plain and cheap plastic ornaments for each year's experiment. We tried loading up a basket with ornaments, but it tipped when Megan stood on her tiptoes to reach high branches. Folding up the bottom of Megan's sweatshirt like a basket worked fairly well, until she needed two hands to fasten a baby Jesus to a branch.

We lost two ornaments that year. After that, the ideas kept getting sillier and sillier.

Rick jokingly considered applying for a patent for his last invention, the sweater hanger. He lined the inside front of an oversized sweater he had bought at a used clothing store with a heavy piece of plastic, secured with black electrical tape, to create a protective barrier. Then, he and Megan attached little wire hangers to each of the ornaments and hung six of them on the front of the sweater. She looked like a human Christmas tree.

"Economy of labor," Rick had said. "I'm all about making life easier."

This year will be the first time Megan will tackle the trimming on her own.

"Why don't you wait until Ben wakes up and see if he'll help?" I say.

Neither of us believes that will happen, so I take another approach, hoping to save the house from my little hurricane.

"How about you open one tin of ornaments at a time? Hang them, then put all the packing paper back inside when you're done."

Megan rolls her eyes at me.

"You know me, Mom."

"Consider that an ornament order," I say, tapping her nose with my finger.

Megan finishes her breakfast and returns to her room to complete a "secret project," while I make a list of unfinished holiday chores before going to the office. Christmas Eve is approaching, and I still haven't given my family an affirmative on hosting the celebration here like I usually do. I've been shopping shy ever since I abandoned my cart in the bicycle aisle the other day.

"Tonight, you return to toy land," I tell myself. "Or, maybe ease back into shopping at one of the stores on the outer rim of the mall."

Nick has wrestling practice tonight and Megan, basketball. That leaves me three hours of freedom after work. I need to buy Megan a new Christmas sweater, and I have furnishings to purchase for Nick's new room. I leave a question mark on my list behind Ben's name. Rick had planned to buy him seat covers for his car. Now that I've confiscated his keys, I think it prudent to come up with another gift idea.

❄

The newspaper office is quiet with only three of us working.

I write a story about added law enforcement on the highways over the holidays. Police departments and the state highway patrol also don't shut down for the holidays, so I easily reach post commanders and local police chiefs. I wrap up the article in under two hours hoping to go home, but my editor hands me another assignment.

"Have fun with this one," he says

With the turn of the century twelve days away, he has asked me to piece together an account of Dayton on New Year's Day 1900.

I find everything I need in the newspaper archives. Local celebrations were simple family gatherings, no big party where people came to cheer at 12:01 a.m. I like that idea; it seems that families haven't changed all that much in one hundred years.

The weather was the big news story of the day back then. Frigid temperatures had turned the Great Miami River into a thick sheet of ice that had beckoned skaters and sleighs. I imagine women with hair coiffed high in the Gibson-girl style sliding across the ice with suited gents in bowler hats.

My siblings and I skated on that same stretch of river every winter when we were kids. I remember walking stiff-legged for days after an afternoon on the bumpy, frozen water. There were no Zambonis to smooth the surface, and I ended on my backside more often than up on my skates.

The only time I truly enjoyed being on the ice was when Rick glided beside me, holding me upright. Secure in his arms, I could float across the ice like an Olympian. That's how I drifted through life until his death, always leaning and holding on tight. Now I am learning to skate on my own. I know there are still bumpy patches, but I am not alone. I'm excited about the possibilities.

I finish writing the historical piece with a feat of gallantry involving a runaway team of horses hitched to a wagon with no driver at the reins. Passersby marveled as a spectator leaped astride the galloping team and brought them under control. Reading people's accounts of the moment, they describe it as something out of a story rather than real life. Heroes don't jump on runaway horses anymore, I think to myself; they leave anonymous gifts on doorsteps.

The drama reminds me of our true friends and the promise I made to the kids last night. I call Gem City trying to track down a home telephone number for Terry. The operator won't give it out, but promises to leave him a message. I put in a call to Tom, thinking he may know how to contact our old friend. I get his answering machine.

I stop at home to change into jeans and gym shoes before shopping. The house is dark, so I flip the switch by the door and the tree lights illuminate the room. I expect to see our pine bedazzled with tinsel, baubles, and beads, but it's as naked as when I left this morning.

It's clear its state of undress isn't from a lack of effort.

Ransacked ornament tins clutter the living room with wads of packing paper spilling from open lids. Glass balls are arranged on the coffee table by color: red, green, silver, gold. Folks unfamiliar with my Megan might think she's trying to organize them.

Not my little girl.

She's searching for something.

From the appearance of the room, she hasn't found it. I get the step stool from the garage and carry it down to the family room closet. I know what she's looking for and where to find it. I'm standing on tiptoe, feeling around, when my fingers touch the edge of the metal tin on the top shelf labeled "Precious." I scoot it across the wooden surface until I can grab it with both hands.

Running my fingers across the cold surface of the lid, I study the picture stamped on top: a white stone castle built for King Ludwig II of Bavaria, the very one used as a model for the Disneyland castle. The tin had been filled with chocolate-dipped cookies, a gift to Rick from a Gem City Engineering customer. The cookies didn't last long, but the beautiful tin has become very special to me.

I return to the living room and plant the box and myself near the tree.

The container holds my family's Christmas history, each year individually wrapped in white tissue paper. A bewildered bride and groom stand side by side on a ceramic ornament, with "Our first Christmas together" and "1980" stamped in gold letters. A baby boy in red pajamas tangled in light strings smiles from the 1982 ball that commemorates Ben's birth. There's a tiny playpen with a teddy bear dated 1987 for Nick, and Megan's rocking horse is inscribed 1989.

My mother bought them all for us over the years. The Christmas after my dad died, she told me why.

"Give these to your children someday to hang on their own Christmas trees. They will be grown, and I will be a memory. Tell them these are from Baci and Grandpa Huist. Tell them they were loved even before they were born."

I'm tempted to hang these keepsakes on the tree myself, but set them aside to leave for Megan, with my supervision. I have told her the story of these precious keepsakes. I will tell her again, while she cleans up this mess, and then we can hang them together.

I change my clothes as planned, grab my purse, and head for the door. The mall is waiting. My kids need presents. I am just stepping onto the porch when I see a car rounding the bend up the street.

"Wait a minute," I say out loud.

The vehicle looks similar to the one we chased the other night.

No time to close the door or turn off the lights. I stand my ground and stare as it passes. The car doesn't stop, but I imagine that the passenger is slumping down in the front seat, like I did.

When the car turns the corner, I shift into high gear, figuring they'll circle the block and return in a few minutes. I run outside and pull my Grand Am into the garage, then turn off the lights in the house so it looks like no one is home. I am crouching on the living room floor next to the front window with my binoculars aimed at the street, when my hair gets tangled on a low-hanging branch of the Christmas tree.

"Crap."

I yank at my hair, which luckily comes loose, but the tree nearly topples.

I thank goodness that I didn't put our special ornaments on the tree.

I give up my hazardous hideout, a twig still knotted in my hair, and run up to Nick's bedroom, where I hope to find a better vantage point. I reach his window in time to see a lone figure step from a car more than a block up the street.

A small figure moves quickly up the street toward the house, growing larger with each step. The dark-clad creature crisscrosses yards staying in the shadows, and I lose sight of it more than once. The figure disappears again somewhere in the flower bed that borders our house.

I'm swelling with emotions. Our gift giver is standing below this window, waiting to step onto the porch where a beam of moonlight will reveal his or her identity to me.

Seconds pass with no movement. I hesitate, think about running downstairs and opening the door, but I don't want to take my eyes off the porch. Flattening my body against the wall, I try to get a better view. I pull myself up to straddle the rim of an old dog food bucket that holds Nick's Lego collection. Balancing on the thin edge of plastic I peek out the corner of the window. My sweaty palms clutch at the wall for a handhold. I test the stability of the curtain rod, but it is already loose. My heart is thumping, and I think of Rick, but this time I am not afraid. I am too excited. The view is much better up here. I can see someone moving around the boxwood.

The mysterious figure steps out of the shadows . . . and I fall down.

I catch the flash of a smile before I tumble into Lego land.

I bang my head on the frame of Nick's waterbed, and my backside lands on hundreds of building bricks. Laughter bubbles up from somewhere deep. I try to stop, but it's a runaway.

"It's got to be the bump on my head," I think, rubbing the blossoming lump, which hurts. "Or, maybe I am happy."

The feeling warms me like holding a new baby, or hot soup on a winter day. I imagine my coworkers, the kids, or even Rick seeing me sprawled on the floor. He would be laughing the loudest. I would be laughing with him.

That's what I do. Lie there on the floor laughing. I can't seem to stop.

When I regain composure enough to stand, the street is empty. The car up the street has moved on, but our Ninth Day of Christmas gift is waiting for me. As I walk downstairs to retrieve it, I try to picture the face that glanced up at me.

It was a woman, definitely a girl. Or maybe a teenage boy. Perhaps an older man or a midget. Admitting I have no idea makes me laugh all the more. The wisp of a smile does confirm to me that our true friend heard me fall, or feels good about giving.

I'm ready to feel that way, too.

I walk out the door without a coat. I have presents to buy. I don't stop to look inside the gift bag on the porch—time enough to do that later as a family.

My kids will have Christmas, and if I learn the identity of my smiling friend, I'll make sure the holiday is special for all of us. I arrive at the mall an hour before closing and whip through stores like a reformed Scrooge.

I buy three outfits for Meg, including a new red sweater.

Nick gets baggy blue jeans and sweats. I buy new running shoes for Ben, plus snow boots for everybody. The weight of the shopping bags gives my biceps a workout, and it feels wonderful.

A little girl trailing her mom around the shoe department approaches me at the checkout counter.

"Lady, you have Christmas tree in your hair," she says.

Sure enough, I am wearing a twig.

My spree at the mall ends when a department store clerk asks me to leave.

"We're closing," she says.

No bother. I have to collect my kids. No time tonight to buy a bed for Nick or whatever else Megan and Ben want. I am Christmas delayed, but I will make up for the weeks I lost. I will be ready by December 25.

A new and improved mom picks up Nick and Megan from their sports practices. I itch to quiz them about items on their Christmas lists.

"No problem," Nick says pulling a notebook from his backpack. "What kind of money are we talking about?"

Megan hasn't made a list yet, so her brother gives her a sheet of paper and encourages her to get started. When Megan asks if I've been Christmas shopping this evening, it feels good to answer truthfully, "Lots."

When we arrive home the gift is missing from the porch, but the lights of the tree brighten the window. Ben must be inside. His siblings and I burst through the door asking questions.

"Where is it? Did we get a gift?"

Ben points to the dining room table where he has added nine votive candles to our centerpiece. The table is set with our Christmas china. In the kitchen, a pot of spaghetti simmers on the stove. The culinary arts class he took at the high school is paying off.

"You've been busy, Ben."

"Dinner is served, Momma."

I will always remember this meal, the first truly happy one since before Rick's death. We illuminate our dinner with candle and Christmas tree lights. Ben tells us about a new video game he's been playing at Robert's, and I make a mental note to buy it for him. I tell my children about the story I wrote today and the runaway horses. We all agree to go ice-skating on New Year's Day.

Before the last spaghetti noodle is slurped, we decide to host the big family gathering at our house on Christmas Eve, just like always.

I'm so caught up in the meal and conversation that I forget to ask Ben if our true friends left a card. I remember later, after Megan and Nick have cleared away the packing debris from the living room floor.

"I mean, I think we got a card. I didn't read it. I went straight for the candles, then I got the idea to make dinner. I threw the bag on the floor with the rest of the mess."

Ben searches through the trash while I empty each of the ornament tins. I find candy canes left over from last year, a spare house key, and someone's baby tooth, but no card. Ben also comes up empty-handed.

"Another mystery?" he asks.

Robbed of a chance to look for clues on the card, Nick is upset over the loss.

"We haven't solved the first mystery yet," Nick complains. "We're never going to find out who the gifts are from."

Megan tells him not to worry.

"I know what the card said. Want me to sing it?"

Her sibling is not amused.

Megan sticks her tongue out at her brother and starts putting hooks into the ornaments she left on the coffee table. When she gets seven attached to her sweater, she walks over to the tree and plots the locations each will hang.

Ben gets the honor of placing our toilet-paper-roll angel on the top and then sprawls on the couch, pointing out bare spots in the branches that need Megan's attention. I find perfect perches for each of our special ornaments. When the tree is fully dressed, we match tins with lids and return them to the basement closet. Our now-empty heirloom tin will remain under the tree until after Christmas. Inside it rests the cards from our gift givers—at least the ones we can find—safely stowed inside sheet protectors, now forever part of our family's Christmas history.

While in the basement, I pack away our painting supplies and peek into Nick's new room. It is nearly ready for occupancy. The walls are painted and the carpet cleaned.

It just needs furniture.

Nick heads up to his old room with the intent of starting the transition.

From his room, I hear him shout.

"Who's been messing with my Legos?"'

Chapter Ten

The Tenth Day of Christmas

The next morning, the kids are still snoring as I lock the front door behind me. I arrive at the office by seven a.m. and then skip lunch. Eight hours later, I am waving good-bye to coworkers, guilt-free. I have Christmas shopping to finish, and I want to be home in time for dinner.

This trip to the discount store is meant to be a quick one, as I still need to buy a bike for Nick. I pull into the parking lot and head toward the shopping cart corral, when something inside a nearby car causes me to stop midstep. The fading December sun illuminates the contents of the station wagon, creating a rainbow of dancing colors on its windows. One glance inside the wagon, and my shopping ambitions morph into criminal intent.

There on the front passenger seat, holding court over an assortment of shopping bags, is the identical twin to our poinsettia, the one left by our still-mysterious true friends on the porch on the First Day of Christmas. I know I shouldn't be loitering in the parking lot, attempting to break into the car parked next to mine. But the matching wrapping paper on the two plants could be my first solid clue to the identity of the gift givers. All of the lessons I had learned reading Nancy Drew amateur detective novels in elementary school are clicking into gear.

I take a slow scan around the parking lot, making sure no one is watching, then I jiggle the door handle of the station wagon a second time . . . just to be certain.

Of course it's locked.

I drag my fingers through my hair and feel sweat beading at my temples, though the temperature outside is near freezing.

I need to find a way into this car.

Knowing where the poinsettias were purchased could reveal so much about the identity of our true friends. If the buy was made in Bellbrook, I can eliminate Rick's coworkers and mine as suspects. None of them live in our south Dayton suburb. Certainly, they wouldn't risk getting caught shopping for the poinsettia in our tiny town, not if they really wanted to keep their identity hidden.

If the Christmas flowers are from the same store here in town, then Megan's Girl Scout troop or someone from the schools will soar to the top of my suspect list.

I just need a look at the price tag.

I pull up the hood of my coat to shield my face from passersby and take a closer look inside the car. With my nose pressed against the window, I can see the white sticker on the pot.

The clue is so close, but it might as well be on the other side of eternity with Rick. I can't read the name of the store on the sticker. All of my rational thoughts, like the fact that I'm about to commit a crime, disappear. All I can think about is the truth and that the possibility of learning it is sitting right there, almost within reach.

I'm tugging at the car door handle a third time, rather violently, when two young men approach.

"Can we help you?"

My hands fly up like a criminal caught as I turn to face two blue-vested store employees. I never saw them coming. My car keys leap from my opening palm and strike one of the fellows on the foot.

My only audible comment, "You scared the shit out of me."

Megan's reprimanding voice screams in my head for use of this four-letter word, and I wonder how I'll tell my daughter her mom will be spending Christmas in the slammer.

The key-bludgeoned clerk picks up the projectile from the pavement, noting the Pontiac key chain, clearly not matching the Volvo I stand beside.

"So, you're not locked out of *your* car. Manager saw everything. Got it on video."

So, their manager had observed my antics on the store's surveillance system and assumed I was locked out of my car, an alibi killed by that blasted key chain. Fear takes over me, and suddenly words are flying out of my mouth

"My husband died . . . my children are devastated. We're getting these anonymous gifts and I have to find out who they're from. . . ."

When they don't immediately respond, I keep babbling.

"The poinsettia in this car, I need to know what store it came from. I *need* to know."

The two men stand there looking at me, then at each other, then at the Volvo. A crowd has started to gather around us. I'm so embarrassed.

"We should probably go get a manager," the young clerk holding my keys says. But that's not what he does. Instead, he walks over to the car and looks inside.

"Not one of ours," he proclaims after eyeing the plant. "All of our small poinsettias are wrapped in green paper."

"I got one from Kroger," a lady from the crowd calls out. "Let me have a look."

As people start jostling toward the window, it seems that everyone in the gathering has bought a poinsettia this season, and they all want a chance to see if theirs matches the one in the car. They all want to help me solve the mystery. One by one they peer in and shake their heads; no one recognizes where the plant is from.

The clerk with my car keys approaches me again.

"I've gotta get back inside. Promise you won't do something stupid, like break a car window?"

I promise and he tosses me the keys. I hate giving up, but I've got to buy that bike and get home. The kids are waiting for me.

As I head to get a cart from the corral, an older woman pushing a cart full of poinsettias—there have to be at least ten—passes me, and I turn to see her destination. When she stops at the Volvo, I turn around.

She's rearranging boxes of poinsettias in the rear of the station wagon to make room for more when I approach her. I hadn't even noticed all the ones in the back.

"Excuse me, can we talk for a minute?"

"If you're after money, honey, haven't got any," she says, picking up her pace. I can tell she's nervous; she thinks perhaps I am unbalanced.

"I just need to talk," I try to reassure her. "I need to ask you about that poinsettia plant on the front car seat. My husband just passed away. I know this doesn't quite make sense. But please."

She rubs the ring on her left hand and her expression softens. I help her load the rest of her flowers into the back of the car.

"I could use a cup of coffee," she says, slamming the hatch door. "How about you buy."

We drive separately over to Frisch's across the street and meet in a booth in the back of the restaurant. She orders coffee, and I get a Diet Coke.

"I don't know where to start," I tell her, ashamed that I'm pulling her away from her own family, her life.

She calls the waitress back to the table.

"Better bring a slice of pumpkin pie with that coffee."

I tell her about Rick, our kids, the gifts. She listens. She nods. She drinks her coffee and eats the pie.

"At first, I wanted nothing to do with the gifts. I even considered reporting our true friends to the police," I confess. "Now, I desperately want to thank them for gluing my family back together."

When I ask her about the poinsettia on the front seat of her car, she responds with a story of her own. She tells me about Neal, her husband, who lives in a nursing home.

"Senility. It's an ugly word," she says. " 'Permanently forgetful' seems less harsh."

She's taking the poinsettias, all of the poinsettias, to the nursing home on Christmas Eve to decorate her husband's room. It's their wedding anniversary. She began purchasing the flowers more than a week ago, patronizing at least seven different stores.

"I'm sorry. I'm not sure where that one came from," she says. "I've purchased fifty-two of them. One for every year of our marriage. It's a tradition Neal started for me on our first anniversary. Every year, he added another poinsettia. Now I'm carrying on the tradition for him."

Her revelation both touches my heart and breaks it. What would it be like to see Rick, but for him not to remember me? All of those years together, all of those memories lost. I grab a napkin to catch a tear, and she tells me not to be sad.

"On Christmas Eve, I will fill his room with those happy flowers. I will feed Neal turkey and mashed potatoes. When visiting hours are over, I'll tuck blankets around him, kiss him good night, and drive home alone. He will forget who brought the flowers, the meal, even my name, but he'll know that someone cares. That's enough for Neal. It's enough for me. It can be enough for you, too."

Then she stands, puts on her red wool coat, and walks away, saying with a smile, "Don't forget to leave the waitress a tip."

An hour later I'm pulling into the driveway at home with two unassembled mountain bikes in the trunk of my car, one blue and one pink. Megan's knees were hitting her handlebars last summer. I know they will both love touring the neighborhood on these. I hide them under a tarp in the garage and hope Tom feels up to the challenge on Christmas Eve of assembling them. If not, the kids and I will figure them out.

Inside the house, I find Megan rearranging ornaments on the Christmas tree. Nick sprawls across the couch with his Game Boy in hand, as Ben works in the kitchen heating up soup for our dinner. He pulls garlic rolls from the oven and announces, "Time to eat."

Seated around the dining room table, in between spoonfuls of chicken noodle soup, conversation naturally flows back to the gift givers. This afternoon I realized that along with the last gift from our true friends on Christmas Eve, my family will be getting something even better: we'll finally meet them. It's a certainty I feel in my gut. It'll be the twelfth and final day—and the perfect way to end their season of giving.

"They'll be here. I just know it," I tell the kids. My faith works its magic on them.

"It could be awkward, if we don't know them," Ben says. "We should plan something."

So we do.

When our true friends pay their final visit, a feast will follow their Big Reveal.

"Cupcakes with sprinkles," Megan suggests the first menu item.

Nick wants chips and chocolate. Ben retrieves my recipe file from the kitchen and places it on the table in front of me.

"This occasion calls for the big guns," he explains.

I sift through the recipe folder, pulling out cards iced with food and finger smudges from holidays past. We decide that our table should be decked with traditional Christmas fare and Old World favorites passed down from my Polish and Hungarian grandmothers. I intend to wow our guests with cabbage rolls and apricot horns. With roasted turkey and pies and cheesecake. A meal doesn't seem like much compared to the way their generosity transformed our lives, but I don't know what else to offer them. People so full of kindness, without cause, must be worth knowing. And feeding.

With the menu set, I decide not to wait until the morning to shop. If we're going to get everything ready in time, I have to start baking this evening. When I stand to clear the table, Ben takes the bowls from my hands.

"I've got this," he says. "I'll have the kitchen cleared for action by the time you get home."

I don't argue.

"Nick and Megan, you've got grocery duty with Mom."

The kids don't question their big brother's authority. No one is more surprised than me. Nick and Megan pull their coats from the closet, sending hangers flying in their race to be the first at the door, but before we leave, there's one more topic I want to discuss with my children.

We have been obsessing over the identity of our true friends. But after meeting Neal's wife—she never told me her name—it isn't such a big deal. She was right: we feel loved, and that's what counts. Even if it is mysteriously from afar.

I look each of my kids in the eyes, making sure I have their attention.

"No more peeking through curtains. No more climbing on the roof."

We all agree. We'll stop trying to catch our friends and wait until they are ready to step forward. I don't think it will be long.

❄

At the grocery store, I have a dilemma: I don't know how many people to expect Christmas Eve. It could be one additional person, but it could also be twenty.

Since my childhood, I have been part of a night-before-Christmas gathering of aunts, uncles, and cousins. We don't come together to exchange gifts. We gather to eat. Following Polish tradition, we wait for the appearance of the first star before sitting down to dinner, no easy feat on a cloudy winter's evening in the Midwest. One year, when dinner had overreached its ready point, my grandmother stepped outside to accomplish what her twelve grandchildren couldn't on an overcast night. She immediately spotted a distant light in the sky and declared it a star. Although I'm pretty sure it was an airplane, her declaration that it was time to eat was welcomed.

Since my marriage to Rick in 1980, I have carried on the family tradition in our home, including his brother Tom's family in the group. Up until a week ago, I had been considering canceling the event. I'm glad I didn't, but the possible addition of the gift givers creates this new problem.

I have no idea how much food to prepare.

Meg dodges shoppers swarming the baking goods aisle, grabbing ingredients from shelves for her great-grandmother's apricot cookie recipe. She's moving quickly, anxious to return home to check for our tenth gift. I'm excited about it, too, but my earlier shopping fiascos have left me with an abundance of last-minute errands.

"I've got the jam. Got flour."

Megan dumps the items into the shopping cart and races off

in search of cottage cheese for the cookie dough mixture, her ponytail swaying as she skips away. I love how excited she is; as a kid, I couldn't wait for my mom to pull these delicate pastries from the oven. I am forever willing to risk a blister for a mouthful of their buttery goodness.

"Yummm . . . these cookies are so delicious," I announce to shoppers trapped beside me in a shopping cart jam.

"Maybe you could share that recipe with my wife," an elderly man whispers as he passes me, with a faux grimace. "She's making fruitcake."

I head over to the meat section of the grocery where I find folks standing three deep in front of refrigerated mountains of ground beef and sausage. I need six pounds of each. Just to be safe, I'm tripling the cabbage roll recipe.

Meg rejoins me there, nearly staggering under the weight of jars of olives, four bricks of cheese, and two jars of pickles—sweet and dill. Clamped under each arm are rolls of sugar cookie dough.

"We're making Great-Grandma's cookies," I remind her. "We don't need sugar cookie dough."

"Couldn't find the cottage cheese," she shrugs, changing the subject. "I found these, though." She pulls two dented boxes of candy canes from the waistband of her sweat pants. She looks at the cart hopefully, and I nod my consent. I've committed to buying Megan's candy canes, but I make a mental note to put back the sugar cookie dough. With a turkey to roast and pies to bake, the flow into the oven will be nonstop through Christmas Eve. As much as the kids like them, I won't have time for the sugar cookies.

We rendezvous with Nick in the snack aisle. He lumbers down the lane pushing a child-sized shopping cart.

"Don't say a word," he warns his sister. "It was the only empty cart in the store."

Surveying the contents of his cart, an assortment of chips and dip, I see what he intends to eat Christmas Eve.

"I'm good," Nick announces. "We can go now. I want to get home and check for a gift."

Megan, too, pleads for home, but I am determined. I will not leave the grocery until all items are crossed off my list.

I am stymied over the selection of a turkey. "What's the problem, Mom?" Megan asks.

Reaching into the freezer case for a twenty-five-pound bird, I wonder if it'll fit in my oven. I shift over to a twelve-pounder, when the image of a dozen carolers knocking on our door gives me pause. They'll sing "The Twelve Days of Christmas." After the final "partridge in a pear tree" rings out and they take credit for the gifts, I'll invite them in to share a meal, but I will have to watch over every bite they take because there'll be a one-pound limit on each guest's turkey consumption.

"I really don't know how big a bird to buy," I fret, looking at my ten-year-old for guidance.

"That's easy," Meg says. "Buy the biggest one."

Nick rolls his eyes, "We're going to need another cart." He heads to the parking lot to pounce on the first available one.

Before leaving the store, Megan spots a Food for Friends bin and asks if we might share with the less fortunate. We pull six items from each of our two carts—cans of peaches and pears, chocolate pudding, and juice boxes.

"The people who get this food, will they know it's from us?" Megan asks.

I shake my head, "No."

"Just like our true friends," she says. "We don't know who they are."

"Just like our true friends," I agree. Megan beams.

"It's the giving that makes you feel good," I tell her.

"Then our gift givers must feel great," she says.

We stuff the trunk of the car with a ham, the turkey, veggies, Nick's chips and dip, the ingredients for mini cheesecakes, cabbage rolls, corn casserole, the apricot cookies, and four rolls of sugar cookie dough, which had mysteriously reappeared in our cart at the checkout.

As we near home, Nick and Megan's attention gravitates to the possibility of a gift waiting to be opened.

"I wonder what they'll leave tonight," Megan says. "Drive faster, Mom."

We're surprised to find our welcome mat empty. The living room curtains are spread wide, and the white lights on our Christmas tree cast a warm glow through the window. Ben stands at the front door waiting for us, an even more welcoming sight to me than the gifts. I suspect his presence at home may have kept our gift givers at bay, but I keep that thought to myself. He meets us at the car and helps to carry in the groceries.

"You plan on opening your own store?" he asks with a chuckle, after a third trip to the car.

Inside, I see Ben has set up a workstation for himself in a corner of the kitchen. A rolling pin, sifter, measuring cups, and wooden spoons are arranged on a card table. Our eight Christmas cookie cutters are there, too.

"Did you remember the dough?" he asks Megan.

She's already digging through the grocery bags.

"I want to thank them, too," Ben says to me, then rips open a roll of dough with a knife. "Like you said, make Christmas merrier for someone else."

Hearing his plan makes me feel like such a proud momma. I set down an armful of groceries on the counter and give him a hug.

In minutes the kitchen and the kids are covered in flour. The first batch of cookies we declare "experimental" when four rows of Santa boots merge into one giant cookie.

"Looks like one of Dad's shoes," Nick says.

Rick wore a size 14AAA.

We all laugh, then laugh again at our own laughter. I think we're all feeling a little guilty over our burst of holiday joy, but grateful for it at the same time.

"Maybe it's a sign," Megan says.

"Of what?" Nick demands.

"That we should eat it," I jump in to cut off any potential argument, breaking off pieces of the giant shoe and passing them around. The second batch of boots turns out better, elf sized.

By the time I'm ready to make cabbage rolls, Megan and Ben scatter to clean their bedrooms, and Nick continues packing up his stuff for the move to the basement. I tackle the raw meat on my own. I am peeling layers of steaming cabbage off a head when the room goes dark.

"Megan . . . I can't cook what I can't see!"

The lights go back on, but in a few minutes they flicker off again. This time a flashlight beam shines on the counter where I am working.

"Megan!"

"They won't come if they think we're home!"

"Close the curtains. It'll be fine," I reassure her. "Now, roll up your sleeves and come play in this meat with me."

"Looks like worms," she says, digging in up to her elbows. When she begins singing "The Twelve Days of Christmas," I hum along. Singing is still hard.

On a beach in Maui on our honeymoon, Rick had burst into song, our song—"Longer," by Dan Fogelberg.

I thought he would stop after the first few lines. It was kind of corny, but he was being serious. He was my one-line comedian, not a musician. At least he had selected an isolated section of beach for his show. And he just kept singing.

"That was my wedding gift to you," Rick said at the conclusion of the song, but even then I could feel his mirth bubbling up. "This is my gift to you, a musical-comedy life."

Then he grabbed my hand so tight I couldn't break free and raced us into the waves together. I was wearing a new linen dress. He had on suit pants.

That was the beginning of our silly, happy, off-key life. When Megan stumbles over the words of the Christmas carol, mixing her ladies dancing with leaping lords, I know I have a choice to make. I can dwell on past songs sung, or I can live here in the moment and sing with my daughter.

I choose to sing with her, but instead of the traditional pear tree and partridges, turtledoves and golden rings, I substitute our gifts, one Christmas flower, two bags of bows, and three rolls of gift wrap.

Sometime during the fifth or sixth chorus, our true friends leave a tenth gift. Ben discovers the package later that night while carrying out bags of trash from his room to the bins on the side of the house. A fierce wind blows outside, and the lightweight parcel had been skipping across our lawn.

"It's here. I've got it," Ben announces, when he reenters the house. His words draw all of us to the living room.

"I was worried," Megan says. "I don't want the presents to stop. I don't want the song to end."

I'm not ready for that either. I wonder if the gift giver heard Megan and me singing. I wonder if they realize their magic is working. Megan tears open the present to find ten dancing Santa paper dolls. We don't try to dissect the card or look for clues. Instead, we hang the paper dolls from the banister and get back to preparing for Christmas Eve.

Returning to the kitchen, I add the new gift to our version of the song and keep on rolling cabbage balls.

On the tenth day of Christmas your true friends give to you:
Ten dancing Santas
Nine Christmas candles
Eight cookie cutters
Seven golden apples
Six holiday cups
Five angel gift cards
Four gift boxes
Three rolls of gift wrap
Two bags of bows
and
A poinsettia for all of you.

Chapter Eleven

The Eleventh Day of Christmas

On the day before Christmas Eve, I wake up with a list of errands already dancing through my head. We had been up late the night before, cooking and prepping food for our party, but no amount of sleep deprivation can dull my excitement. As I weave through traffic thick as winter snow, I swear the Christmas rush is the very best time to shop. The traffic congestion allows me more time to tune in to Christmas songs on the car radio. When I hear John Denver and the Muppets singing "The Twelve Days of Christmas," I feel as if they are crooning the carol just for me.

"Maybe I'll wait until the last minute every year," I say to myself, as I wave a car into a parking space that I had been waiting to occupy.

I find another spot farther out and revel in the brisk air as

I hike into the computer store. I'm replacing the dinosaur Nick has been playing video games on for the past three years, a computer my friend Kate gave to the family after she replaced hers with an updated model. I know my middle child will be thrilled with top-of-the-line technology, but he's going to have to share it with the rest of us. I can't afford to buy more than one. The new model will go in the family room. Even though it provides solitary entertainment, whoever is on it will be in the same room as the rest of us.

No more isolation, at least not from each other.

At the computer store, I meet an elderly man scratching his head over which video-game system to buy for his thirteen-year-old grandson. The clerks are all busy, so he asks me. Vying for the attention of a member of the sales staff myself, I nearly dismiss the guy with "haven't a clue," when I realize I know someone who could help him.

I dig my cell phone out of my purse and call Nick. I hand the man my phone, and he walks off with it toward the video games, as directed by Nick.

I can hear my son say, "She won't mind."

I follow my phone.

Fifteen minutes later the guy is headed to the checkout lanes, and I return to an even longer line of customers waiting to speak with a clerk about a computer.

Before leaving the store, the gentleman tracks me down again and tries to press a twenty dollar bill into my hand for Nick.

"Not necessary," I say. "Merry Christmas to you and your grandson."

"I figured you would say that. At least take this."

He gives me a coupon for a free cup of coffee.

"Have one on me."

The gentleman leaves me ferreting through rows of monitors and motherboards. I hate to admit that I know far less than the average teenager about computer operating systems, and I think about calling Nick again, but I want this present to be a surprise. So, I resign myself to wait for a salesman.

It happens quicker than I expect.

"I saw you helping the old guy. I was with another customer," the clerk says. "Thank you."

Then he yawns while rubbing his eyes and says, "Sorry. We've been so busy. I dreamed we ran out of stock last night and people were pelting me with mouse pads."

"Christmas will be here and gone before you know it," I say. "Try to enjoy it."

"Coffee would help," he smiles, adding there's none left in the break room. "Now, how can I help you?"

The clerk helps me select a hard drive, nineteen-inch monitor, color printer, scanner, and a stash of video games for all three of my children. My purchases will be delivered to Tom and Charlotte's house before noon tomorrow; they will sneak them over after our Christmas Eve celebration, when the kids are in bed.

"You actually bought a computer, and it's on the delivery schedule. That's fantastic, Jo! But you're not just thinking about buying one thing, right?" Char asks, when I call her from the store to confirm the delivery time. "What about the bike?"

When I tell her that two are hidden in the garage, she bellows out a loud, "Thank goodness. When did all this happen?"

"Let's just say our true friends have inspired me."

Charlotte laughs.

"Those gifts have made a difference," she says. "I'll tell Tom to take a nap Christmas Eve. Sounds like the two of you are going to be up late."

When I exit the store, snowflakes are painting cars a glittery white.

"It feels like Christmas," I think. I'm not sure if it's the snow or the shopping that makes me feel this way. I wonder if our true friends will leave footprints in the snow tonight, and whether we will be able to learn more about them based on the size of their shoes. I stop and remind myself that discovering their identity isn't a priority anymore. I just want to thank them.

Instead of driving directly to the furniture store to buy Nick's bed, I stop at a coffee shop. I'm pretty certain beverages are frowned upon in the computer store, but I use the free coupon to get a cup for the weary clerk anyway. Sneaking it inside under my coat, I get the man's attention and hand it to him behind a stack of boxed monitors.

"You're an angel," he exclaims.

I wave off the compliment and leave.

Crossing off the computer from Nick's wish list, I drive three blocks to a discount furniture store. As I walk in and start looking at the prices, I whisper thank you to the folks at Gem City Engineering who are making this possible.

I select a dark chocolate-colored chest of drawers and matching nightstand for Nick, along with a mattress, box spring, and a bed frame.

My son's waterbed will be history by Christmas.

The charge for the furniture is already on my Visa when the salesman tells me, "No deliveries until after Christmas."

I hear him, but my brain—or maybe it's my heart—refuses to accept. This fresh start is all my son wants for Christmas, except for the computer and the bike, and I tell the salesman so.

"My son's father died on a waterbed. He can't sleep on his anymore. . . . He's having nightmares. I've got to move him out of that room."

I don't even remember leaning across the counter and grabbing hold of the guy's tie. When I do realize what I'm doing, I pat the tie as if smoothing it out and back off.

By then others are watching . . . again.

"You should have come in sooner," the salesman tells me, and his tone feels like he's scolding me. "Our delivery schedule is full up for tomorrow."

That old familiar feeling of letting a kid down eats at my conscience. The guy is right. I should have been here sooner. Hearing him say it feels like a punch in the gut after we've come so far, and I am not about to let him spoil my son's Christmas.

And there are others on my side.

A woman in a faux-leopard coat waving a MasterCard doesn't appreciate the comment.

"Her boy lost his daddy. You need to help her."

"Have a heart, buddy," a male customer adds. "Didn't you have a dad?"

"Well, yeah," the salesman says, laughing at the question.

"I thought so," the man says pounding on the counter like he's discovered the answer to one of life's great mysteries. "So, what are you going to do about this?"

The MasterCard lady doesn't give the salesman a chance to answer.

"How about I take my charge card, and I drive over to the

mattress shop up the street to buy a bed," she says, ripping up her invoice.

She points to the gentleman who also holds a sales slip in his hand and asks, "Are you with me?"

He hesitates for a moment, then says, "Sure. Why the heck not."

Two more customers threaten to cancel their orders, and that's enough to make the manager take me aside. He asks me to have a seat in the closeout-furniture section surrounded by an assortment of mismatched, damaged, and out-of-style sale items. There are no other customers in the area, and I get the idea that's why he selected this location. I feel like I have landed on the Island of Misfit Toys, like in the animated *Rudolph the Red-Nosed Reindeer* that's been on television every holiday season since I was a kid.

The manager launches into a spiel about his daughter not getting the Millennium Princess Barbie doll she wants for Christmas because he's been working nonstop since Thanksgiving. I think he is setting me up to soften the blow, and tears start rolling down my cheeks. But then I hear him say, "So I'll make it happen, okay?"

"What?"

"December 24, eight a.m.," he promises. "I'll drop the order off myself."

I hug the guy before leaving the store. I'd like to think the spirit of the season inspires the man, not a mother's tears, threats from customers, or my promise to pay double the delivery fee.

Outside, the MasterCard lady is waiting for me. My smile

broadcasts that all is well, and I thank her for the role she played in getting my purchase on the delivery schedule for tomorrow.

"Most fun I've had in years," she says. "We widows have to stick together."

"You've lost your husband, too?"

"Christmas Day 1990. Keeled over in a bowl of mashed potatoes."

I don't know how to respond to that, other than "I'm sorry."

"The point is, I moved on. I'm happy. Remarried," she says, flashing the diamond on her left hand. "There is life after a death, if you've got the guts to live it. The way you grabbed that sales clerk's tie, honey, you've got it."

A balding guy, maybe seventy, jumps out of a sedan and opens the car door for my new friend. She waves as they pull out of the parking lot. I marvel at how casually she was able to share her story and wonder if I will be like her in a decade or so. While I can't imagine myself remarried, I do hope I have the courage to step up and share what I have learned with others in need.

I have spent the months since Rick's death inside a bubble of grief and fear. But in these last eleven days, as I venture outside that protective cocoon, I have met such a hodgepodge of wonderful people: Goodwill Charles, the soldier at Ponderosa, Neal's wife with the poinsettias, and now the MasterCard lady—every one of them teachers on this new journey I am traveling. They are experts in the art of moving on, forgiving mistakes, and celebrating memories even if they hurt. I still have so much to learn.

I cross Nick's furnishings off my list and drive back to Bellbrook. I still have presents to buy, but now it is time to get the kids involved. Today, I will honor the request of Rick's coworkers and let each of them select a special gift.

The boys lobby to shop at an electronics store. Megan agrees, but doesn't show the same level of excitement as her brothers. We're walking out the door when she asks me to wait a minute. She runs up to her room and comes back downstairs with a small backpack, which she loops over her shoulders.

"What have you got there?" I ask.

"Tell ya later."

Inside the store, Ben takes off to browse, while Nick drags Megan and me to a display of televisions. While I tell each of the kids the gift they select must be reasonably priced, Nick goes straight to a $1,000 plasma flat screen. Rather than get upset, I just laugh.

"It won't fit in the car. Besides, we can't afford it."

We settle on a nineteen-inch set for his bedroom.

"It'll do," he says approvingly.

We find Ben talking to a salesman about a stereo system for his car.

"Uh . . . I kind of blew my speakers the other night," he tells me.

"You may not be getting the keys back for a while."

He shrugs and turns up the dial on the display model.

"This is what I want," he says. "It'll give me something to look forward to."

With the boys' selections made, we meander the aisles with Megan. We show her video games, an electronic diary, a purple karaoke machine. She's not interested. This little girl, who tossed a bag of socks across the family room one Christmas because it wasn't a Barbie doll, can find nothing she wants.

She snuggles close to me as we walk. When Ben tries to excite her with a handheld, video basketball game, she doesn't respond.

"What gives?" he asks.

"Remember how Daddy always went shopping on Christmas Eve morning and brought home lunch for all of us?" she says. "He got his shopping done in under two hours."

Megan stops walking and asks me, "Can I please take Daddy a present? I brought it along in my backpack."

I have not mentioned her dad all day, hoping to stoke this holiday glow we've been building. Maybe that wasn't my best idea. While I visit Rick's grave at least once a week, I have not taken the kids since the funeral. I go there to talk to my husband, and to cry. That's not the ending I want for this day.

Ben takes the decision out of my hands.

"Let's go together, Mom," he says. Nick agrees.

We pay for our purchases and make Calvary Cemetery our destination. As we walk out to the car, I vow to make another shopping trip myself to select a special gift for Megan.

"We won't stay long," I say, driving the winding lanes of the cemetery past crypts guarded by stone angels and rows of headstones marked BELOVED.

Colorful poinsettias and Christmas wreaths with red bows don't have the same welcoming effect here that they have on a house, church, or a store where life bubbles around them. As the snow turns to a chilly rain, fading ribbons and freezing blooms give the place an unloved and lonely look.

Almost immediately I regret coming here.

Megan steps solemnly from the car and walks over to the gravestone marked THE BIG DAD.

Etched on the marble is a mountain with a brook bouncing over stones below it. I selected this design because it reminded me of a clearing where we stopped to rest in Glacier National Park in 1993.

"This is where I want to spend eternity," Rick had said, marveling at the wild beauty and solitude of our perch.

It was not long after that serene moment that we realized we were lost. Our leisurely hike turned into a nine-hour trek through wilderness as we searched for any landmark that could guide us back to civilization. Rick had carried an exhausted, six-year-old Nick on his shoulders and Megan, then four, in his arms, until we found a park ranger station.

We spent nine hours lost in vegetation taller than the littlest among us. Even though we were covered in mosquito bites by the time we returned to our campsite, that wasn't the worst of it. Crossing a rickety suspension bridge over a mountain gorge, single file, traumatized us all a little that day. Dusk was approaching and that was bear country; we couldn't turn back. I crossed first to make sure it was safe. I wanted Rick there with the kids if it wasn't. Once safely on the other side, I sang to Megan as she tiptoed over the swaying expanse. Nick ran. Ben was more cautious, walking slowly, looking down a lot. We held our breaths as the bridge bowed under Rick's weight, but we survived with a heck of a story to tell.

Wind whistles through the bare trees of the cemetery, creating its own eerie music. I'm thinking this is no place for kids two days before Christmas, when Megan pulls from her backpack the seven golden apples given to us by the gift givers.

I had forgotten all about them.

"I want to decorate his tree," she says.

Before Rick died, we had been looking for a larger house in the country, one with some acreage and lots of trees. That was his retirement dream.

After his death, I bought three cemetery plots, a requirement at Calvary to ensure my husband would always have a tree beside his grave. Rick had dreamed of building a home in the country one day, surrounded by pin oaks, walnuts, and maples. He never realized that dream, but I made sure he would rest eternally in the shade.

Megan offers us each an apple to place on the tree. The newly planted gingko is little more than a sapling, but our apples are small, and the branches hold their weight. Though I had my doubts about coming here, it feels good to include Rick in the holidays, even in this small way.

"They're perfect," Ben says.

As the apples sway in the wind, my daughter begins telling her dad the story of the gift givers. We all join in recounting the Christmas mystery as if he were standing here listening. We tell him about Nick's escapades on the roof, chasing the car, and the feast we plan to share with our true friends on Christmas Eve. Nick adds my exploits in his bedroom atop a tipsy Lego bucket to the story.

"Mom had a lump on her head the size of a golf ball," he says, though I declare it was hardly the size of a small gumball.

It has only been a day, and already the tale is growing. It feels right to be here sharing this story with Rick. We are moving on, healing, but we will never forget him.

Megan is singing "The Twelve Days of Christmas" as we

walk back to the car. Nick finishes the carol by adding stanzas with extravagant eleventh- and twelfth-day gifts, including the plasma television and a computer.

The drive home is quiet, but no one is crying. I think we're all tired from the day of shopping. It's good to know that we can visit Rick's grave together and talk to him without the cold grip of anguish following us home.

A few blocks from the house, Ben sees a neighbor struggling to pull a Christmas tree out of the back of his minivan.

"Slow down, Mom."

My eldest rolls down the car window and calls out, "Need a hand?"

I am so proud that I reach over and hug him.

"If there's a gift at home don't open it without me," he says, climbing out of the car.

Our true friends were indeed bold today, leaving a package on our porch in the middle of the day. We don't peek inside until Ben returns. Our eleventh gift turns out to be the most tasteful: a plateful of eleven edible mice wait to be nibbled. There are even bits of cheese scattered around the plate.

The creatures are made of chocolate-dipped maraschino cherries and Hershey's Kisses, and each has two almond slivers for ears. Their eyes and noses are painted on with icing.

"They're so cute. We shouldn't eat them," Megan says.

I pop one into my mouth. It's a sweet treat to revive us after the long day out. Then three sets of hands are grabbing their share. Before I think to write down exactly how they were made, the mice become history. Each of the kids had gobbled three, and I ate the other two.

This time we don't forget to pull the card out of the package. It's another elaborate one, with a Christmas tree adorned with maroon-colored ornaments.

"The decorations on the card look just like ones hanging on our tree," Nick says.

"That's uncanny," I say.

"Na, they probably just saw them from the window."

I read the card out loud this time.

On the eleventh day of Christmas
your true friends give to you . . .
Eleven hungry mice
Ten dancing Santas
Nine candles
Eight cookie cutters
Seven golden apples
Six holiday cups
Five angel gift cards
Four gift boxes
Three rolls of gift wrap
Two bags of bows
and,
One poinsettia for all of you.

"Rats," Megan says, devouring bits of cheese from the plate. "Wish we had more mice."

Chapter Twelve
The Twelfth Day of Christmas

A dreary gray mist hides houses and holiday decorations early Christmas Eve morning, like a theater curtain before the opening of a play. I suspect our gift givers will want to spend Christmas Eve with their own families, so I rise at dawn to put our oversized bird into the oven. I want the turkey juicy and golden before noon, in case they put in a lunchtime appearance.

"Just a few hours until showtime," I say to myself, after rising before six a.m. because I'm too excited to sleep. Tree lights will twinkle, the table will be set, and our true friends will step onto the stage.

It seems ages since the first gift magically appeared on our porch, that rain-soaked little poinsettia our first guidepost toward healing. Could our gift givers have known just how much we needed their presence, or did they have any idea how much they had given us this year?

I walk upstairs to find Megan awake and already keeping watch for them by the living room window beside the tree. A plate of the apricot horn cookies sits on her lap, and there's one in her hand.

"Cookies for breakfast . . . really?" I ruffle her hair and join her by the window.

"These babies have apricots, eggs, and cottage cheese baked into them. That's not a half-bad breakfast."

"And the sugar?"

"I'm going to need energy today. You better have one, too," she says, waving a treat close to my mouth. My willpower melts, and I snap off a bite. When she reaches for another cookie, I take the plate and fetch bowls of cereal from the kitchen.

The turkey goes into the oven first, and then I transfer the cabbage rolls from the refrigerator into my mom's vintage Westinghouse Roaster Oven, where they'll simmer all day.

I wash and Megan dries our assortment of Christmas plates, platters, and bowls, then we stack them on the sideboard.

We arrange trays of homemade fudge and cookies on the plates, covering them with plastic wrap to keep them fresh. In between tasks, Megan checks the porch. The sun has only just risen, and I expect our gift givers may still be in bed.

"Give them time," I tell her. "You don't want them to catch you in pajamas. Go get dressed."

Megan is halfway up the stairs, when she reaches over the banister and flips the switch on a string of tiny lights wrapped around the railing and a swag of fresh pine, a last minute purchase.

"I never thought I'd say this, but I wish Christmas would

wait a couple of days," she says. "Do you suppose they feel the same way?"

"Well, we didn't make it easy for them, always watching from the windows. They're probably looking forward to a rest."

Nick wakes when the aromas wafting from the kitchen seep under his bedroom door.

"Must eat turkey," he says, pretending to sleepwalk.

"Not for another four hours," I tell him. "Just popped it in the oven."

"Wake me up when it's ready," he says, but my boy doesn't go back to bed. Instead, he stands on the steps, closes his eyes, and savors the scents of our Christmas. Megan and I do the same, just as our friend in the military had described.

I had wondered which holiday memories my kids would carry into adulthood. Now I know at least one that they will. Nick breaks the magic of the quiet moment.

"Smells pretty good, but it doesn't beat presents."

The mention of presents sends both him and Megan racing to the front door.

No visitors yet, but the door hinges are getting a good workout. It's the sixth time we've checked the porch this morning, and it's not even eight o'clock.

Nick sits down at the dining room table, surveying the progress Megan and I have been making on our Christmas Eve celebration. He decides to help. Though he casts off my request to place silverware in the caddy on the table, he does retrieve the potato chips from the cupboard. Figuring his intent, like his sister's, is to eat junk food for breakfast, I stop him before he rips open the bags.

"Keep them sealed until after our company arrives," I say. "Otherwise they'll be gone before anyone gets here."

He calls me Scrooge but eats the cereal I place before him. Megan takes a break and sits down with her brother. They are conjuring images of our gift givers.

"Has to be somebody with ninja skills," Nick says. "Nobody can escape unseen as often as they did without superhuman strength and speed."

The doorbell rings at 8:01. I spot the truck from the furniture store in the driveway and order Nick upstairs to take a shower. His special-delivery bedroom has arrived.

My eldest hears the doorbell and hurries up the steps from the basement still buttoning his shirt. The store manager is alone on the truck, so I volunteer Ben to help him.

While the guys maneuver the queen-sized box spring down the stairwell and around my new pine swag, I sneak around the side of the house and leave a package on the seat of the delivery truck. I'm back in the house before they notice my absence.

"You happy now?" the store manager asks before departing.

I hand him a plate of our homemade Christmas cookies, and he's munching one as he steps up into the cab of the truck. A few minutes later, he's ringing the doorbell again, a Millennium Barbie under his arm.

The tag on the box says, "Merry Christmas, from a friend."

I open the door just a smidgen and shoo him back to the truck.

"Get your work done and go home," I say.

"Thank you." He smiles. "I'm sorry I thought you were crazy."

❄

The mantel clock chimes four p.m., and the turkey sits on top of the stove drying out. The plastic wrap is off the cookies, and one bag of chips has already been consumed.

I have never been more prepared for Christmas. All we need are guests.

"So this is how it feels to have a party and no one comes," Nick says.

It's time for accolades, toasts, and congratulations on a job well done, and we have no one to give them to. Our true friends have been hard at work for eleven days. Surely, they'll show up for the paycheck, a thank-you.

"It's early yet," I say with an eye on the window. "Baci will be here at six p.m., and Uncle Tom, Aunt Char, Uncle Ron, Aunt Lori . . . all of your cousins. It's going to be great. Everyone will meet them."

By five o'clock, Ben is pacing the house, and his brother is continually banging the front door. We take turns in the shower, so there is always a set of eyes on the porch.

As twilight begins cloaking our little town, we flip on the tree lights, set the oven on warm, and we wait.

Ben seeks me out in the kitchen, where Nick and Megan won't hear us.

"They've done so much for us. Why stop now?"

I take hold of his hand, and we join his siblings, seated on the floor by the tree. This is a conversation I want to have with all of them.

I start at the beginning, with our first gift.

"I was so angry over the loss of your dad. When the poinsettia arrived, I wanted to throw it away. I couldn't face buying a tree or decorating. I wanted to hide my head under a blanket. Our true friends wouldn't let me."

Megan is able to better articulate what I'm trying to say.

"You don't get so many colds, anymore. And I got this beautiful tree. I'm grateful to the gift givers."

"We don't need them so much anymore, not like we did in the beginning. We have each other. We're going to be okay."

"Well, thank goodness for that," Nick says. "I was worried for a while."

Megan breaks the circle and runs up to her room, and Ben hurries down to the basement. They return with gifts.

"Don't you want us to wait until tomorrow to open these," I ask.

Ben and Megan look at each other and answer, "Nope."

Megan distributes her carefully wrapped homemade artwork, and we hang them on the tree, until after the holidays. Ben gives Nick the comic books and his sister the game. They are wrapped in newspaper comics.

"The basketball hoop, uh, cost about the same as a pound of butter and a gallon of milk," Ben admits.

Megan lunges at her brother and gives him a bear hug.

I think Nick is embarrassed because he has no gifts to give. He grabs three bags of chips off the dining room table and tosses one to each of us.

"Said it yourself, Mom. Small gifts can make a difference," he says.

Ben gives me an enlarged photo of our family, all five of us.

When he sees my eyes glistening, he sets it on the mantel and asks everyone to pose in front of the tree for a new one.

"Next year's present," he says. "I'm thinking ahead."

Everyone jumps when the doorbells rings. For the first time today, there were no eyes on the door.

With a hand on the doorknob, I whisper instructions.

"I'll open the door on a count of three, then everyone shout 'Merry Christmas.' One . . . two . . . three."

The plan works perfectly.

My eighty-year-old mother, their Baci, is so startled she jumps backward. My nieces Andrea and Melissa luckily prevent her from falling.

"What a welcome!" Baci says. "Merry Christmas to all of you."

The arrival of relatives and the horde of presents they carry momentarily distracts everyone. By the time my sister Lori along with her sons Nicholas and Tony arrive, the house is humming with conversation and laughter. Megan, Nick, and Ben fill our family in on what's been going on with our mysterious gifts, explaining that we are sure tonight will be the night that all will be revealed. Everyone wants to be part of our Secret Santa experience, and they all have questions.

Baci demands to see the gifts and mourns the fact that there are no more mice.

"What time do the gifts usually arrive?" ask their cousins Jim and Mike, who set up a lookout on the side of the house with Ben.

When Tom pulls his truck into the driveway, a dozen sets of eyes are watching him from the window.

"Are we late?" Charlotte asks. "What's going on?"

I give her an update.

"They'll be here," Charlotte says confidently, and I wonder again whether she knows more than she has been letting on.

With so many of us on the lookout, I move away from the window to tidy the snack table. I wipe up spills, pick up crumbs, nibble on veggies and cookies. I delay dinner, because I don't want to be caught in the middle of a meal when our true friends arrive. I want them to sit down with us.

Just before eight o'clock, Baci decides it's time to eat.

"The first star came out an hour ago," she says. "It's tradition. I need food."

We gather around the dining room table laden with homemade Polish sausage, my cabbage rolls, traditional ham and turkey, plus all the trimmings.

Baci instructs everyone to join hands, and she leads us in a very quick prayer of thanks for our feast.

"It would have been longer if we'd eaten an hour ago," Lori whispers. "She must really be hungry."

I silently ask God to bless all of our family, including those who are not here to share this meal with us. I give thanks for small gifts and true friends.

Later, after consuming multiple plates of meat, salads, and casseroles, two mini cheesecakes, a piece of fudge, and a generous serving of her aunt Mary's peanut butter pie, Megan skedaddles over to my seat and plops on my lap.

She whispers in my ear, giggling.

"Do you suppose our gift giver could be someone sitting here at the table?"

Scanning the room I see only faces of people who love us, and I realize how lucky we are to be surrounded by family.

"They're all gift givers," I tell her. "We can be, too."

I wrap my hands around my daughter, and she lays her head on my shoulder, the scent of peanut butter pie sweetening her breath. I savor the moment surrounded by family, delicious food, and festive decorations, and wonder if Rick sees what I see.

"Rest easy my love," I tell him silently. "All is well."

Just after ten, Ben announces, "a butt load of cars just pulled up across the street!" and we all crowd around the front door. Sure enough, a few cars are parking along our block.

"This is it," I say.

Megan jumps up and down beside me. The whole family gathers on either side of the tree. The lights of the car nearest our house turn off, and we wait for the driver to step out. I am holding my breath as the car door opens. Nick shines a flashlight out the picture window for a first glimpse at our guests.

Rick's eldest brother, David; his wife, Dorothy; and their five children are walking across the yard toward the house. From the other cars, Dorothy's mother, sister, and her family emerge. A collective sigh of disappointment from our group of nearly twenty rings across the room—it is not some mysterious stranger. We laugh at our own reaction. Everyone except Ben, Nick, Megan, and I go back to eating.

We usually spend Christmas Day with David's family, so I wasn't expecting to see them tonight. We will have dinner with them tomorrow.

"This can't be a coincidence," I say.

The kids clearly have the same idea. Megan rushes her aunt as she walks in the door. "We love our gifts," Megan says.

Dorothy laughs. "I haven't given them to you yet. David, get the presents out of the car."

"Then, it wasn't you?" I ask.

My sister-in-law gives me a puzzled look. I recount our tale of true friends.

"It wasn't us, but I wish it had been," she says. "We just thought tonight would be hard for you. That's why we're here."

How wrong I had been to think we were alone that year. We are surrounded by love, and I am grateful to everyone who reached out to us. The house is positively bursting. Young cousins open presents and speculate about what they will find under the tree in the morning. I serve drinks, make sandwiches, and load plates with slices of pumpkin pie. I quiz all of our late arrivals about the twelve days, but I'm so busy making sure everyone is fed and comfortable that I'm hardly worried about it. I love being in hostess mode, to see the food I prepared be enjoyed, to have the house filled with love, to feel part of a family.

It is nearly midnight when the last of our guests say good night, and things have slowed down enough for me to realize that our gift givers never materialized.

"Just be thankful for their effort," Charlotte says, before leaving. "Your true friends obviously wanted you to have a Merry Christmas, and you are."

Ben, Nick, and Megan open one gift each before going to bed—new pajamas—a tradition in our family since they were toddlers. Megan curls up on the couch and closes her eyes, but she refuses to go to bed.

"Maybe the gift givers will come tomorrow," she says.

I answer, "Hope so."

"Well, they remind me of Santa Claus. Maybe this is just something we're supposed to believe in, like a miracle."

I don't think she's far from the truth.

"This is how legends begin," I say.

I plant a kiss on her cheek and point her in the direction of her bed.

"It's cool having our own family legend," Nick says, following her up the stairs. "Somebody ought to write a book about it."

Uncle Tom and his computer-literate son, Tommy, return an hour later to assemble the computer system and a new desk. Ben helps them while I busy myself wrapping presents. I lay out the holiday paper, scissors, and tape on the living room floor where I can still keep an eye on the window. I remember Megan sitting by her wide-open window, asking our true friends to stop bringing the gifts that she feared were painful for me even though they meant so much to her—it was just a few nights earlier, but already it feels like so long ago. Now, I crack open the window just a sliver so I will hear any activity on the porch.

I wrap a basketball for my daughter, the boots, videos, and lots of blue jeans and sweaters. I shove Nick's television into an extra-large trash bag and tie bows around it. Ben's car stereo fits snugly into a gift bag. Because she loves to sing so much, I had gone back to the electronics store and bought the karaoke machine for Megan.

"Get some rest," Tom says, surveying the avalanche of presents threatening to crash down on Nick's electric train, which is still chugging around the tree.

Sometime after four thirty a.m., I fall asleep sitting upright on the living room couch, still hoping that our anonymous elves will appear.

Chimes from the bells of St. Francis Church drift in through the open window, waking me on a beautiful Christmas morning. The sun I have longed to see for weeks shines today, and the world outside my window is painted with a thin coating of snow.

I am tired and don't want to move off the couch, but I have to look. Wrapping an afghan around my nightgown, I step outside.

There are no footprints in the snow, no twelfth gift waiting.

The disappointment is striking, a blow.

I return to the house, close the window, and curl back onto the couch.

Is it selfish of me to want more?

Our true friends gave us kindness, unsolicited, but desperately needed. Their gifts were a sign that even our shattered home could be put back together—with community, with family, and with love. They had given us back Christmas, and each other. Our true friends had broken the hold grief had on us and gave us an extraordinary experience during a holiday season that otherwise would have been bleak. They had given us our own Christmas legend, as Nick had called it, a modern-day miracle. That's a lot to accomplish in twelve days. Was this precious lesson the twelfth gift?

I throw off my blanket, slip into my robe, and turn on the tree lights. Two weeks ago I couldn't face the holidays; now I can't wait for the kids to wake up. At last, I understand the message our gift givers sent. I just needed time to figure it out.

I flip on the oven, light a burner on the stove, and plug in the waffle iron in one fluid motion, then grab eggs, ham, and a tube of cinnamon rolls from the fridge. Bella begs to go outside, so I oblige while reading the directions on the back of a box of Belgian waffle mix.

I glance out the kitchen window when our dog starts howling, generally a sign Bella wants back in the house, or there's a full moon. She is sitting on the back deck next to something, but her body is partially blocking my view.

I run out the door in my bathrobe and slippers. An artificial pine, less than a foot tall, sits on the deck. The tree is trimmed in brass bells. I don't bother to count the ornaments as I carry the little tree inside. I know there are twelve.

I remove the pine-scented candle from the table and make this little tree our new centerpiece. My hands tremble as I open the card.

On the Twelfth Day of Christmas
Your true friends give to you . . .
Twelve Brass Bells
Eleven Christmas Mice
Ten Dancing Santas
Nine Candles
Eight Cookie Cutters
Seven Golden Apples
Six Holiday Cups
Five Angel Note Cards

Four Gift Boxes
Three Rolls of Gift Wrap
Two Bags of Bows
And
One Poinsettia
For All Of You.

I find another message on the back.

"We hope in some way we have made your Christmas a little easier. Someone did this for us once. You are in our thoughts and prayers."

The note was signed "Your friends."

I sit down at the table weak with realization. Throughout these last few months, our pain had been paramount. I had imagined our gift givers as generous people, but ones who were happy and whole, strangers to loss.

How silly of me.

They knew the power of the twelve gifts because they had endured the same pain. Their compassion for us had grown from a deep knowledge of the sweetness and sorrow of the season, when joy and grief intertwine.

I am warmed by the idea that someone helped them survive it, just as they had helped us. I imagine the legacy of the gift givers stretching back over centuries to the very origin of the song and beyond.

Next year, it will be our turn to sing, our turn to carry on this tradition of kindness and giving.

Perhaps it's the scent of the cinnamon rolls that wakes my children. I'd like to think it part of our Christmas miracle that they appear at that moment. I can feel the tears pricking my eyes as I hug them each, but today they are tears of joy. I lead them to the table and show them our beautiful little tree.

"I want to tell you the story of the thirteenth gift," I say.

They gather around me and listen.

Chapter Thirteen

The 13th Gift

The magic of that Christmas stays with us today, many years later. Retelling the tale of the thirteen gifts is as much a part of our family tradition as trimming the tree.

Seated around the dining room table that morning in 1999, Ben, Nick, Megan, and I had committed our lives to carrying forward the lessons of our gift givers, but in our own special way.

Everyday can be Christmas. Megan came up with that motto.

I never stopped searching for the identity of the gift givers whose kindness helped my family to heal. They had given us new memories and a very special holiday tradition, but I still felt stuck, unable to fully move on without knowing who they were.

I needed to thank them.

I had long suspected my sister-in-law Dorothy knew more about this mystery than she let on. Could she and David have deposited the tree with twelve brass bells on the back deck, while all eyes were focused on the front of the house?

Over the years, I had questioned Dorothy, but she declared her ignorance time and again.

At a family gathering in the summer of 2013, I asked her one more time. I told her my desire to share our story so others could learn the lessons that had so benefited us. When she tried to change the subject, I didn't let up like I usually do. I couldn't.

With her elbows on the picnic table and her face in her hands, she obviously was conflicted. I could also tell she knew the truth.

"Please," I said. "I need to meet them."

She took a deep breath, and then, she surprised me.

"I'll ask them if it's okay," she said.

I did a little happy dance there under the awning, surrounded by submarine sandwiches, birthday cake, and family.

"This means so much to me," I said.

We cried together that day, but just a little. I didn't know who our gift givers were—yet—but my arms were extended, and the golden rings were finally within reach again. I felt giddy and nervous, but hopeful that these generous friends would grant my wish.

A few weeks later, I got a brief telephone message at work from Dorothy.

Our true friends now had names: Susan and George Armstrong of Kettering, a community not far from where we lived in Bellbrook. They had lived only a few miles away all these years. Had we passed each other in checkout lanes, met at the gas pumps, dined in the same restaurants? I saw their goodness in everyone I met.

With their identity revealed, I couldn't wait to see their faces.

On a sunny Saturday in March 2014, Nick and I met them face to face to share a cup of coffee and conversation. Sweet, kind, generous, and funny, they are treasures. Susan is a retired social worker, and George, a retired high school art teacher. Now in their midsixties, the couple has played Secret Santa to twenty-two grieving families, with help from their children: Noah, Zachary, and Natalie. Our family was the ninth to benefit from their healing generosity. In recent years their grandson Jackson also has joined their elf pack.

"Why us?" I asked.

Susan told me that she and my sister-in-law have been lifelong friends. She had known Rick's family since he was a skinny second grader.

"I just remember him as this cute little kid running around the yard," Susan said. "When we heard that he had died, we decided right away that we wanted to do this for his family."

"We couldn't believe someone so vivacious could be gone," George added.

The images Nick and Megan conjured of the gift givers having ninja skills weren't far off the mark. While Susan or George drove the getaway car, their kids dressed as ninjas or G.I. Joes, running across lawns, jumping fences, sometimes crawling on their bellies to avoid detection. Their parents would wait up the street with the car motor running and doors open so their children could jump in quickly.

It was their daughter Natalie, then age seven, whose face I saw smiling up at me through the window of Nick's bedroom right before I fell. We didn't find our twelfth gift until

Christmas morning, but Zachary had deposited it on the back deck the night before. Our lookouts had made his job difficult.

"He had to cut across yards and sneak around the back of the house," George said. "It seemed like we waited forever for him."

As for the clues on the cards we tried so hard to decipher, there weren't any, only healing words.

"How did you know exactly what we needed?" I asked.

That is when Susie told me that their tradition of holiday gift giving had begun as a way to honor the short life of a baby daughter and sibling, Andrea Erin Armstrong.

"I woke up feeling funny, like I wasn't pregnant anymore, even though I was due in two weeks," Susan told me. "A good friend was going to have a baby shower for me that day, but I knew something wasn't right."

Susan delivered Andrea on September 29, 1989, stillborn. Andrea would have been twenty-five in 2014, the same age as my Megan.

"I still think about her every day," her mom said.

Christmas hit the Armstrong family hard that year, just as it did us after Rick passed away. Then, thirteen days before the holiday, a poinsettia mysteriously appeared at their home.

Small gifts followed for twelve days, each with a card echoing "The Twelve Days of Christmas" song. Noah was nine years old that Christmas, and Zachary, five. Their reaction to the gifts was similar to Ben, Nick, and Megan's.

"I'd be feeling low, and then a gift would come and it would take my mind off our loss for a while," Susan said. "It was day three or four before we realized this was going to go on for some time."

The joy the gifts brought to the family extended beyond the holidays. The next year, as a tribute to baby Andrea, Susan and George decided to play Secret Santa themselves following the tradition set by their true friends. Originally, the couple selected families who had lost infants as they had. They expanded their giving to include other losses because they saw the need. The tradition for Andrea continues.

"Her life was short, but we learned so much from her. We wanted her life to make a difference," Susan told me over coffee.

As parents, we teach our kids to walk and talk, ride bikes, play games. The Armstrongs passed on to their children a legacy of goodness and giving. What an amazing heirloom.

"They were all I could ever have imagined and more," Nick said, after meeting the couple.

Most of the families that they visited never learned the identity of their true friends. I feel lucky to shake their hands and say thank you. I also wanted to know why the secrecy was so important to their giving.

"The premise was always to take away the pain. We hoped the mystery would provide some relief, especially if there were children involved," Susan said. "We didn't want people to know it was us. This wasn't about us. It was about the families and the devastating loss they were facing."

Nick and I drove away from the meeting with George and Susan smiling and energized, but with one nagging question. The members of the Armstrong family were second-generation gift givers. Now, we wanted to know who started the tradition.

"We would never have thought to do this on our own," Susan had said.

It had taken me thirteen years to track down our gift givers. The trail of clues leading to the Armstrongs' true friends dated back to 1989. I told myself it didn't matter, that I should be satisfied knowing the ending of our story. But it did matter.

Once again, the Armstrongs guided me.

Though they didn't realize it until the twelfth day, the Armstrongs had known their gift givers. All those years ago, when Susan had sought answers after Andrea's death, she had left a message on a perinatal helpline at Miami Valley Hospital.

An expert in grieving had called her back, and the two women became friends.

Sue Hundt wasn't then college trained in counseling or psychology, but she had been one of the first volunteers to answer the helpline when the hospital launched the service in 1987. She and husband Ron were well-known at the hospital after eight pregnancies, including two sets of twin boys.

Only two of their children had survived.

"You don't have any training for grief. It just happens, so you've got to feel your way," Ron said. "We felt we had a strong story to tell, that there is a light at the end of the tunnel. There are ways to survive that awful moment."

It was Ron, a city planner and artist, who came up with the concept to use "The Twelve Days of Christmas" carol. He is Santa Claus. The Hundts began their annual Twelve Days of Christmas tradition in 1988, and they have never missed a season.

Today, their family includes son Adam, adopted daughter

Marilee, and Mollee. As with the Armstrongs, the Hundt children are all veterans in the Secret Santa tradition.

"So many people helped us grieve after the loss of our twins; they helped us exorcise the demons," Ron said. "We wanted to find a way to give back."

From their own experiences, the couple knew that healing took time; one gift wouldn't be enough.

"We liked the song. We wanted to do something that was drawn out, but simple, that could involve their kids if we could," Sue said. "Part of the fun has been parking the car up the street and waiting to see them open the door and find the gift."

Now a special needs teacher, Sue was a stay-at-home mom and babysitter in the early years of their giving. Money was tight. She worried about the cost, but Ron reassured her that the gifts didn't have to be expensive.

"The gifts didn't have to be big. It was mostly, what do they need?"

These true friends begin looking in January for a family to visit when the holiday season rolls around. Their church community, coworkers, and the perinatal helpline where Sue still is a volunteer have helped them identify families who have suffered a loss or just need a hand.

The Hundts tailor their gifts to meet the specific needs of each family, such as food, diapers, and toys. On the eleventh day, they leave a Nativity set. The baby Jesus figurine comes on Christmas Eve, when they always reveal themselves.

"This is how I can say our children's lives helped someone else," Sue said.

❄

This Christmas Eve I will gather my grandchildren around me, Ben's Gavin and Gracelynne. In the glow of the tree lights, I will retell the story of the thirteen gifts and show them the homemade cards. Ben, Nick, and Megan will join in the tale, as they always do, embellishing each of our exploits, especially mine. This year, for the first time, the story will have a proper ending.

Meeting these two couples was a blessing. There were no awkward moments. We were friends after all, even before we met. I had always imagined them as superheroes. Learning they, too, had been vulnerable only strengthens that image of them in my mind.

I have walked away from our encounters touched by their happiness. These couples sought new ways to make the holidays matter despite their own heartbreak. Through them, I learned how to celebrate the season while keeping Rick's memory close. The power of their gifts lies in the understanding that joy and sorrow can coexist comfortably and without guilt.

I couldn't help but wonder if their joy in life had been rooted in their good deeds. Recognition for their actions had never been part of their mind-set. Call it giving back or paying it forward, they had taken the kindness shown to them by others as a challenge to live a worthy life.

They have more than met it.

Now it is our turn to try.

We don't all have to become gift givers dashing across darkened lawns in ninja outfits to experience the high that living a generous life can bring. But even in moments of deepest grief, we can turn off self-survival mode and share with others all that we've learned along the way.

Folks have asked me over the years if my children and I became gift givers. I tell them we remain inspired by our true friends, but I leave that mystery for others to solve.

Then, I lure them into a conversation.

I tell them one of the greatest gifts we all possess is the ability to give. Wealth isn't a prerequisite; compassion and a kind heart are all you need. What better way to honor our loved ones, past and present, than to reach out and change a life for the better? And, the holidays are a perfect time to look outside of ourselves and be a true friend. A legacy of generosity can create memories that reverberate beyond the moment and outshine the brightest of heirloom ornaments.

Acknowledgments

This book began many years ago in the pages of my journal, where I felt free to share every dark moment and fear. It took encouragement and support from family members and friends to bring it to life.

Thanks to everyone who helped me through those early difficult times as I struggled to stand on my own as a single parent. Tom and Charlotte, David and Dorothy, Ron and Mary, you guys are the best. To my sisters Carol and Lori, who began supplying me with notebooks and pencils in grade school, you will always be remembered and missed.

My gratitude and love go out to Kate, who coerced me back into college, gave me my first computer, and remains my greatest teacher and friend.

Many thanks to the members of the Key Lime Writers' Group, Janet, Rosalie, and Mary Lou, who dried my tears as I began writing raw with grief. Their gentle prodding and continual feedback compelled me to the keyboard from first chapter to last.

To my former coworker Margo, thank you for listening to me as I worked through this story out loud and then on paper. You had the courage to tell me when I was moving in a wrong direction both with the book and in life; I know it takes a dear friend to do that.

To my agent Hannah Brown Gordon of Foundry Literary & Media: thank you so much for believing in this book. And to Kirsten Neuhaus: thank you for helping to find wonderful homes for this book around the world. To my supporters at Harmony

Books, including publisher Tina Constable, editorial director Diana Baroni, publicist Lauren Cook, marketing director Meredith McGinnis, and all of the sales, production, and promotion teams—I really appreciate your early enthusiasm about what this book could be and now is. To my editor, Leah Miller: you made this writing journey feel effortless, and I am grateful. I also send a huge thanks to the editors and reporters at the *Dayton Daily News,* who pushed me to dig for details, write lean, and tell the truth.

To the Antioch Writers' Workshop, where I found my voice and learned to write creatively, thank you for providing me with opportunities to develop through your workfellow program. Lessons I have gleaned there fill every page of this book.

To my beloved Rick, Ben, Nick, and Megan, along with my grandchildren Gavin and Gracelynne and their mom, Cynthia, thank you for giving me reasons to rejoice in life every day.

Finally, I send out a prayer of hope and gratitude for gift givers everywhere. Your generosity of spirit fuels us all forward.

Joanne Huist Smith
Dayton, Ohio
April 9, 2014

About the Author

Joanne Huist Smith is a native of Dayton, Ohio. She earned a bachelor's degree in English at Wright State University and worked as a reporter for the *Dayton Daily News*. She is the mother of three and grandmother of two.